RABIES
MOM

RABIES
MOM

Jack McGowan and Pat Carroll

Rabies Mom LLC

For further information, please contact:
Jack@RhinosLife.com

Book design by:
Arbor Books Inc.
www.arborbooks.com

Printed in the United States of America

Rabies Mom
Jack McGowan and Pat Carroll

1. Title 2. Author 3. Parenting & Family Issues

Library of Congress Control Number: 2007908336

ISBN 10: 0-9801106-0-2
ISBN 13: 978-0-9801106-0-9

"In the lilt of Irish laughter, you can hear the angels sing."

This book is dedicated to the memory of my daughter,
Shannon Gabrielle Carroll
May 23, 1996–November 2, 2006 (All Souls' Day).

I love you, my sweetheart. I miss you so much.
Until we meet again.

ACKNOWLEDGEMENTS

Thank you to RhinosLife.com for their financial help in making this book a reality. Without them, it would not have been possible.

CHAPTER ONE

I met Jeannine McGraw in 1983 at Chicago's South Side Irish Parade. I was twenty-seven at the time, freshly divorced after a three-year, childless marriage. Jeannine was twenty—though at the time, she said she was twenty-one—and she took my breath away. She was beautiful, full of life and laughter, and I fell in love almost instantly. Within weeks she had moved in with me, and six months later she was pregnant.

The son of Irish immigrants and a good Irish Catholic, I did what I thought was the right thing: I proposed. We were married on St. Patrick's Day in 1984.

Shortly after that, Jeannine started to miss work, calling in sick for any reason she could think of and some days just not showing up. She had a good job at the Palmer House hotel in downtown Chicago, in the catering department. Eventually, she lost the job, but I didn't care. I made enough to provide for our little family and was comfortable with her being a stay-at-home mom, devoting all of her attention and effort to raising our baby.

Every man secretly longs for his first child to be a boy, so when our first son, Peter, was born on June 11, 1984, I was on top of the world. I had a new wife whom I was crazy about, a new, perfect baby boy, a good job at the Chicago Stock Exchange and a beautiful home in Chicago. Things were going better than I ever could dream.

Then, in January of 1985, Jeannine's father passed away. Never very adept at handling tragedy, Jeannine slipped into a deep depression and failed to see the good things in her life. As a new mother, she could not bring herself to find joy in watching her newborn son grow, giggle, and learn. She was too concerned with her own pain and her own loss.

I came home from work one evening to find her sitting on the couch, her arm hanging limply over the armrest. Her glazed eyes were half open and her mouth hung slack, as if she had been given Novocain.

"Are you feeling all right?" I asked.

She rolled her head back and forth slowly, as if it were suddenly too heavy to hold up.

"What's wrong?" I leaned over her to look at her face. She reeked of booze. I glanced around the room and found an empty bottle of gin lying on the floor near the hallway. I felt my face get hot with anger. Drunk! She was drunk while alone with our infant son!

"Nothin'. Jus' sittin'. Waitin'." Her speech was slurred.

"Where's the baby?" I demanded. I could not believe she was so irresponsible.

"He's...fine," Jeannine said, her eyelids drooping closed. I tapped her cheek a few times.

"Jeannine! Where's the baby?"

She slowly opened her eyes. "Shleepin'. Don't worry. He won't remember me."

"What?" Won't remember her? What was she talking about?

She tried to close her eyes again, but I shook her awake. My heart was thundering in my chest.

"He won't remember me. Won't hurt as much for him, the way it hurt for me..." Jeannine said. Her head rolled away from me, her eyes turning to look at the picture of her father, framed and on display on the end table.

"Jeannine, what happened?"

"Took some pills."

"Pills? What pills? On top of the gin?"

"That prescription ibuprofen I had left over from—"

"How many?" One hand on each cheek, I forced her face back toward mine. "Jeannine, how many?"

"Res' of th' bottle."

"Shit!" I leaped over the couch and grabbed the phone to dial my mother-in-law. She was closest. One ring. No answer. "Come on," I whispered to the phone, keeping both eyes fixed on Jeannine. Two rings. Why wouldn't she answer? "Still with me, Jeannine?"

"So…tired," she said. Her voice was faint.

In the middle of the third ring, my mother-in-law answered the phone. I quickly asked her to come over to watch the baby so I could bring Jeannine to the emergency room. She agreed and hung up.

Wasting no time, I ran outside to start up the car. Back inside, I grabbed Jeannine by the waist and hoisted her to her feet.

"Come on, walk around with me."

"No. Too…tired."

I slapped her cheeks to wake her up. "Come on, Jeannine, stay awake. Walk with me."

I brought her outside, hoping the crisp night air would help keep her awake. We walked around the car until her mother arrived. Without even greeting my mother-in-law or waiting for her to get inside the house, I put Jeannine in the car, rolled down the windows and peeled out of the driveway.

We made it in time. Jeannine had her stomach pumped and was admitted to a psychiatric ward for a week. She spent a few days talking to psychiatrists, telling them, in my opinion, exactly what they wanted to hear to get herself discharged. She was supposed to go to follow-up appointments with a therapist, but never went. She did, however, take all of the medication they prescribed for her.

On July 13, 1986, our second son, Mark, was born. Four years later, on August 24, 1990, we had our first daughter, Barbara. In the meantime, Jeannine's widowed mother moved in with us. It was a blessing to have her there. Not only did she help out with the children, but Jeannine seemed to be happy to have her around. Her mother was a comfort to her.

And because of her mother's willingness to babysit, Jeannine had more free time than she'd had in a while. Though she seemed content with hanging around the house, sleeping and doing God knows what while I was out at work all day, I felt that her time could be better spent earning a little money to help us out. I told Jeannine that I wanted her to look for a job, and you would have thought I'd told her to chop off her own hands. The arguments we had about this were monumental, culminating in her first threats of divorce.

Maybe to spite me, or maybe just because it was the first thing that crossed her path, Jeannine signed up for bartending classes— not a job, just classes—from an ad that she saw on the back cover of a matchbook. She stayed with this for a month and was miserable the whole time, making me feel just as bad. She talked about divorce every day, especially when I tried to talk to her about getting some real, meaningful employment or asked how she planned to find a bartending job once she was finished with her training.

By this point, Jeannie's attempted suicide incident was buried under ten years of a life together, and it was all but forgotten. At least, it was never spoken about—Jeannine became far too sensitive and defensive for that, still exhibiting behavior that some people called "eccentric" when they were being polite. We got into a family routine: I would go to work; Jeannine would stay home with the kids. I would come home, drink a six-pack and go to bed; Jeannine would stay up until the wee hours of the morning and finally go to bed around two or three. That was our life.

Since we had moved into our house in Chicago, Jeannine had been convinced it was haunted. Rumor had it that a child had died in our house, but I was never entirely sure if these rumors were actually in circulation or something concocted by Jeannine's imagination.

Jeannine was a big believer in the paranormal, but in this case her fascination had turned to fear. She didn't like to be alone in the house, day or night, and we argued over whether or not to sell it. I didn't believe any spirits resided in the house. It was old. The floorboards creaked and wind whistled outside the windows. I was not about to pick up and move over a few noises, but Jeannine would not let it go.

One rainy night, Jeannine and I were lying in bed; I was sipping my beer and watching TV and she was reading a book. Heavy raindrops battered the windows, the wind whistled and the house was making its usual creaking noises. I was used to it and thought nothing of it.

Jeannine slapped her magazine down on her lap. "Did you hear that?"

"Hear what?"

"That moaning sound."

I didn't look away from the TV. "It's probably the wind."

"Probably," Jeannine said. "Probably—but how do you know? I don't think it's the wind. It sounds like a child."

"It doesn't sound like any of our children. We just checked on them. They're asleep."

"Exactly!" Jeannine said, grabbing my beer away from me to get my full attention. "I think it's that child who was killed here. I think she's crying out for help. I don't like this, Pat. We need to move."

"Jeannine, we've been through this. I'm not going to pick up and move because an old house creaks."

"You said it was the wind."

"I said it was *probably* the wind—could be the house, could be one of the kids talking in their sleep."

"Could be the soul of that child."

Jeannine always had to be right. Her logic was fuzzy at times, but she would argue a point tooth and nail until she was satisfied that she had a decisive victory in the debate.

"Jeannine, we're not moving. I'm tired and half drunk, please…"

"Then we need to do something about it."

"And what do you propose we do?" I asked. "It's an expensive renovation to have new hardwood floors put in."

"At my bartending class, I met this woman named Winter Wren—"

"Winter Wren? Are you kidding me?"

"Yes. She's a psychic and—"

"Oh, Jesus. Jeannine, are you serious?"

"Let me finish!" Jeannine snapped. "I told her about the spirits and she said she and her boyfriend could perform an exorcism on the house!"

"You know I don't believe in any of that crap. Please, go to sleep!"

"Just because you're so narrow-minded doesn't mean that I am, or that these spirits don't exist! I won't be in this house while they're here. What if they try to hurt our kids? Then you'll be sorry you didn't listen to me."

I was not going to win her over on this one. Jeannine had set her mind on this and was beginning to get fired up.

"Are they going to charge us?" I asked.

"No. It's out of the goodness of their hearts."

"What are they going to do? They're not going to do anything to the house, are they?"

"No. Just cast a circle and banish the malevolent spirits."

I sighed. Jeannine, knowing she had won, threw her arms around my neck and kissed me. "They'll be over this weekend."

When our doorbell rang that Sunday afternoon, I answered it. I had to see these people for myself. There, on my doorstep, stood a man and woman probably in their mid-thirties, wearing long, black robes. Both had scraggly hair that fell nearly to their hips and were adorned with beaded jewelry from head to toe. They positively reeked of incense, and I could not help but suspect that it was to cover up the smell of something else.

I gathered up the kids and took them out for the day, so we'd stay out of their way. That evening when I returned, Jeannine claimed that she could "feel" that the spirits—or demons or whatever—were no longer there and that there was less noise in the house. I noticed no change, but didn't argue with her—as long as it made her happy and stopped the incessant arguing.

CHAPTER TWO

After thirty days of constant fighting with Jeannine over her getting a job, I finally couldn't take any more. I folded—I told her that she didn't have to work after all and that she could quit the bartending classes.

This was how it always went with Jeannine: she would pick a fight, we would argue over it for weeks, sometimes, and then I would just give in and tell her what she wanted to hear and apologize for things I didn't even do. I admit that it probably wasn't the best tactic all the time, but she was merciless in her quest to be right. It drained all my energy just to keep up with her craziness. Maybe turning my head and letting her have her way wasn't the best choice, but when you're that worn down, what else can you do?

Miracle of miracles, Jeannine did not mention the divorce again after I told her that she didn't have to work. Things went back to normal almost overnight; we were just a happily married couple again.

In 1995, Jeannine's mother moved out of our house and into a trailer park with her fiancé, all the way out in Portage, Indiana (forty miles away). All of a sudden, Jeannine started hinting that she would maybe like to live there, too, so we went to check out the area.

It was more than I could have hoped for. The schools were

good, and the neighborhood was a far cry from the party atmosphere surrounding Chicago—which we had decided it was time to get away from. Besides, Jeannine wanted to be there, close to her mom.

So we moved.

Jeannine's happiness was always short-lived, however. She was always searching for something *more* and was so concerned with what she lacked that she didn't notice what she had. She was a full-time, stay-at-home mom with three beautiful children. We lived comfortably, but it wasn't enough for Jeannine—nothing ever was.

She had her first extramarital affair that I am aware of in the late fall of 1995.

Jeannine had been feeling depressed and unfulfilled over the summer, so she decided to take a little break from the kids and visit her brother, Jerry, out in California, just in time for his annual Hawaiian luau barbecue. Thirty or so of Jerry's friends were there—among them, Steve, an old rock and roller around Jerry's age. Steve is a nice guy, pretty mellow and is still a good friend of Jerry's. Jeannine really liked him and they enjoyed themselves at the luau. They drank, socialized, swam—and, apparently, had sex in Jerry's hot tub after nearly everyone else had left.

The fling never had an effect on our marriage, mainly because I didn't learn about it until after we were separated. Jeannine returned from California and we continued our life together as usual. A few months later, she became pregnant. Our fourth child, Shannon, was born on May 23, 1996. She was the most beautiful baby I had ever seen. I felt that my family was complete. And with our five-bedroom house, each of the kids could have a separate room.

Jeannine, however, wanted more children. Looking back, I can't help but wonder if that was because she actually wanted to have another baby, or if she just did not want to be pressured into getting a job after all the kids started school. Whenever I tried to address the issue, it led to one fight after another, and I was given the cold shoulder and the silent treatment until I apologized. Jeannine knew me well. She knew exactly how to push my buttons.

By 1999, Jeannine was pregnant again. This time, the pregnancy was much more difficult for her, so she went to several doctors to figure out what was wrong. It was then that she was diagnosed with Crohn's disease, which attacks the small intestine.

As such, her pregnancy was a real threat to her life. Her family pleaded with her not to have the baby, but she refused.

"If I don't survive," she said, "it is God's will."

I feared for her, but after slamming down a few beers, I supported her decision. I could never bring myself to approve of aborting a child, no matter how drunk I was. The doctors gave her the option of being treated with various steroids, but Jeannine's vanity would not allow her to do that. She didn't want to get dark hair in places she had never had it before. She did not want to bulk up with muscles. So she sought out an alternative and found it in New Age medicine. She had done so much research into the medical practice that she even knew about herbal doctors and the differences in treatments.

In April of 2000, we had another beautiful little girl, Mary. Mother and daughter came through just fine.

At that point, I suggested that Jeannine have her tubes tied. She said she would think about it, but before any real decisions were made, she was pregnant again. Once again, her family urged her not to have the baby.

"Who will take care of your kids if something happens to you?" they asked. "What will happen to your family if you end up permanently disabled—or worse?"

I worried about the same thing, but again, could not bring myself to even suggest an abortion. It didn't matter anyway. Jeannine was convinced that if anything happened to her, it was "God's will." And there never was a more stubborn woman.

In December of 2001, Kristine was born. After that, Jeannine had her tubes tied.

A month later, after twenty-nine years of service, I was laid off from my job at the Chicago Stock Exchange. There I was, forty-six years old, with six children, a mortgage, a wife who didn't work, and no job or health insurance. Jeannine and I had very little savings. We were spendaholics. Though I received a compensation package, I knew it wouldn't last long. I was scared stiff and stayed drunk for a whole week.

After the initial shock of losing my job wore off, I would go to downtown Chicago three to four times a week and spend all day on the trading floors, waiting for a job opportunity to present itself. I had to do something to get out of the house. The routine I had followed for twenty-nine years was no longer possible. Now what? Applying for jobs was so different; it was a world I didn't understand. I didn't know what to do. I hadn't felt so helpless since I was twelve years old, when my mother had passed away. I slipped into a depression and was unable to eat or sleep.

Jeannine tried to comfort and console me and asked friends to do the same. She even borrowed money from her brother, Jerry, in an effort to start up a day care.

"Since I'm home with the kids anyway, why shouldn't I just watch other kids? It'll help with the bills."

I loved the idea, so Jeannine got started. She bought all of the necessary things and even took a few classes on how to operate such a business. But she never followed through. Looking back, I think she went through all of that so people would at least *think* she was making an effort to step up to the plate.

In March of 2002, my persistence finally paid off. I found a trading-floor firm that not only was hiring, but started me with a higher base salary than my previous job. Words cannot describe the euphoria I felt. I could eat, sleep and relax again. I could support my family again. The weight on my shoulders lifted and the knot within my stomach unraveled. Things were starting to look up again; I stopped worrying about saving and continued to spend like I used to, but cut back on my drinking a little.

I had a good job again. I had a home, a wife I adored and six children—six beautiful children, all bringing wonder after wonder to my eyes with every step they took, every report card they brought home, every lesson they learned and every laugh they let out.

Jeannine, however, was still not happy. The summer after Kristine was born, she began to complain of horrible back pain, so she started seeing a chiropractor. X-rays showed that she had a bulging disc.

She had weekly appointments and prescription pain killers, but nothing seemed to alleviate the pain. She continued to see the chiropractor on a regular basis, claiming that her various medications were not working. As her dosage increased, so, it seemed, did her complaints of pain. Whenever she was given stronger medication, she would claim it "helped," but the aching never completely went away.

Jeannine consulted a specialist and the subject of surgery came up, but the doctors advised her against it. She was young, and there were too many risks involved in operating that close to the spine. One slip and she could be paralyzed for life. They recommended that she live with the pain on increased medication and continue with outpatient therapy. It was possible, they said, for the disc to heal on its own.

Jeannine opted for the surgery and wasted no opportunity to tell anyone who would listen about how dangerous it was and what the risks were. Attention was showered upon her, and she seemed to revel in it.

After the surgery, she was given a higher prescription dosage. She still complained of back pain and her new, ridiculously high prescription dosages were simply not enough. But there was something else bothering me. Jeannine began to change.

She distanced herself from her family, with whom she had always been close. One by one, she cut off contact with her friends—starting with the ones who knew her best. To question

Jeannine or express concern about any of her idiosyncrasies was an assault as far as she was concerned, and grounds to sever ties. Her oldest friends, the sort who were cherished because they told it straight, without any sugar-coating, were tossed aside for the slightest offense—and Jeannine took offense at everything. The only friends she kept in touch with were the ones who went along with everything she said. To contradict her was the surest way to have her cut you out of her life.

The stronger the pills she took, the more rapidly she spiraled downward, until she was no longer the Jeannine we all knew and loved. She was prescribed and was addicted to methadone, although she has continued to deny it. To this day, she insists that she only took it when she "needed it." It's transformed her into someone I can't understand or feel any sympathy for.

Meanwhile, our arguments became more frequent and heated. They were over little things—the garbage, the laundry, repairs she felt were needed on the house—and usually ignited by Jeannine's quick, defensive temper. I began to smoke a little pot to take the edge off. I was always discreet about it and never let the kids know what I was doing—or, at least, I thought so.

Jeannine's schedule conflicted with mine to such an extent that it was almost as if we were living in different time zones. I was up at five a.m. and in bed by ten at night. She developed a habit of going to bed at two in the morning and sleeping until noon or later. Needless to say, on top of all the other difficulties we were having, our sex life was non-existent.

We should have discussed our differences and sought marriage counseling, but we didn't. We're both to blame for that. It was difficult to discuss anything with her because she saw the slightest criticism as a direct attack against her. She never liked anyone to challenge her. She had to be right. I would get pissed off after our fights and drink until I passed out. This was getting ugly.

CHAPTER THREE

After a long day at work, I pulled into the driveway one evening in September of 2003 and turned the car's engine off. I cracked my neck on either side. Even from inside my car, doors closed, windows up, I could hear music blasting from within the house.

When I opened the front door, it was as if I had walked into a Rolling Stones concert—she'd always been a huge fan of the band. The music was cranked to its maximum volume. The bass shook the windows and the lamps, threatening to blow the speakers. If any of the kids were trying to do their homework, I didn't see how they could get anything done. And there was Jeannine, dancing around the living room, singing along to the music with a dust rag in her hand, occasionally tapping a piece of furniture with it. At least she was in a good mood.

"I-I-I-I can't get no...sa-tis-fac-tion..."

"Jeannine," I said. I couldn't even hear my own voice. "Jeannine!"

She spun around and stopped dancing. She put the dust rag on the entertainment center and turned the music down to a somewhat normal volume.

"Good, you're home. I wanted to tell you something."

I moved in to give her a kiss, but she backed away and gave me a wicked smile. "What's the matter?"

"I'm not happy, Pat. I'm not happy here, with you. And I've been doing a lot of thinking about this... I want a divorce."

The words were said with such casual ease that it didn't sink in at first. She might as well have been telling me she wanted to wear blue tomorrow. Twenty years of marriage and there I was, in my own living room, being told that it was about to end while Mick Jagger sang in the background.

I calmly walked into the kitchen, opened the refrigerator and grabbed a cold beer, then turned around to face her. "I… You can't be serious…"

"I'm very serious. I've thought about this for a long time."

"But…why?"

"I told you. I'm not happy. Don't you think I deserve to be happy?"

"Sure you do, honey." I took a couple of gulps of my beer because I couldn't believe that I was having this conversation. Then, my legs gave way and I sat down on the couch. I put my beer on the coffee table, rested my elbows on my knees and buried my head in my hands. Not happy? With the house? The kids? Me? I loved her. Despite all the recent arguing, I loved her and had always thought this was something we'd work through—a bout of depression Jeannine just needed to overcome.

"Think about what you're doing here. What about the kids? Try to give us a chance. We can work through this. You love me, don't you?"

"You're a no-good, lazy drunk, Pat! You do nothing around the house—"

"I work all day, Jeannine!" was the only comeback I could think of. I couldn't believe she was saying this to me. Sure, I liked to drink a couple beers when I came home from work at night, but I deserved it! After all, I was the only one in that house who was bringing home a paycheck. I got up and went to work every day, provided as good a life as possible for my wife and children and paid all our bills, and I didn't see anything wrong with enjoying my beer and pot when I wanted to. I never did anything crazy in front of my children; inebriated or not, I never did anything to put them in danger. A *no-good, lazy drunk?* That was just a flat-out lie.

"—and you're wasting my time!" she went on, not even listening to what I said. "I deserve a chance to be happy!"

Happy. Happy. Happy. She repeated the word over and over, but never told me exactly what was making her unhappy.

"We agreed when we got married that I would be the bread-winner and you would stay at home with the kids."

"But I need help, Pat. The kids are more than a full-time job."

"Then I'll help out more. Jeannine, I'm begging you. Reconsider. Think of what you're doing, what you're throwing away. Give us a chance. What about marriage counseling?"

"No. I've made up my mind, Pat. I want a divorce." She turned the volume back up on the stereo, picked up her dust rag, and continued to pretend to clean the house. I sat on the couch in the living room, staring at her for a long while. She never looked back at me. I watched my cold beer get warm and threw it away.

Six children including a new baby, nearly twenty years of marriage, a beautiful, five-bedroom house, and Jeannine wanted to toss it all out the window. It was financial suicide for her and it was going to be brutal on our children, but Jeannine could not be reasoned with. She had to be right.

For weeks, I tried to talk Jeannine out of filing for divorce. She would not budge. I pleaded with her, telling her to consider our children and the love we had for each other. I started doing things around the house and being more attentive to Jeannine, and even stopped drinking for a while. But, I still needed a joint every night so that I could relax.

"I don't love you anymore, Pat," she told me one night. "I'm not sure I ever did. This is important to me. I deserve a chance at happiness while I'm still young enough to enjoy my life."

I didn't want to lose her. I loved her, my kids, my life. I was not about to sit back and let this happen.

"Why aren't you happy? What can I change, what can I do to make you happy?" I asked, over and over and over again.

"Nothing. It's just too late. I don't like the way you look and I can't even stand the smell of you! You make me ill."

I begged, pleaded and tried my hardest to get her to reconsider, to find something about our life together that she loved which made her happy. I even said that we could go see a therapist. Finally, she told me how much she loved our house, but her biggest complaint was that the main bathroom was out of date and in need of repair. Some time before, the kids had left the bathtub running, which had resulted in a lot of water damage.

In a desperate, last-ditch effort to make her happy and patch up our marriage, I began to ask my friends and coworkers how much repairing the bathroom would cost, and if they could recommend a good contractor. The general consensus was that it would cost around $15,000, so I applied for a loan at my bank and continued to ask my friends and associates if they knew any reliable remodeling contractors.

Sometime in mid-October, I came home to find Jeannine flipping through magazines, an excited smile on her face. "Good! You're home," she said. "I got a call today from a handyman named Sam Isenberg—he said you know his brother."

Ken Isenberg worked with me at my new job. He had mentioned to me that his brother did some work as a handyman, but since I was looking for a contractor, I didn't pay too much attention.

"Well, he's from Bourbon and said he got our number from his brother. I made an appointment for him to come over and give us an estimate on the bathroom remodel."

"Whoa, whoa, whoa. Back up. I don't like the idea of a handyman. I'd rather hire a licensed contractor so I know he's skilled enough for the job. We might need to get some work done on the plumbing or electric."

"I told him that and he said that he can handle anything like that. And he said that a normal remodeling job, depending on fix-tures and whatnot, should run anywhere between seven and nine thousand dollars. That's almost half the price we expected to pay, so maybe we could get a little more than we planned—like a Jacuzzi. That would feel so good on my back."

"I would just prefer a licensed contractor, so we know he's capable."

"He sounded really good over the phone. Said he had plenty of experience and even has some pictures of jobs he's done. I'm keeping the appointment with him tomorrow."

There would be no arguing with her—especially not with our delicate situation—so I backed down.

The next day, I arrived home from work to find Sam and Jeannine on the couch, reviewing plans for the new bathroom. Sam stood up and shook my hand when I entered the room.

"Mr. Carroll? Sam Isenberg," he said. He was a good-looking kid of medium build; he had a ponytail and was probably in his mid-thirties. He seemed soft-spoken and when we went over our options for the bathroom, he appeared knowledgeable in his trade. He said the job would take two to three weeks maximum and the total price, with a Jacuzzi tub, would be around ten thousand dol-lars.

"Sounds great. Where do I sign?" I said.

Sam shook his head. "Nah. You seem like decent people. I trust you. You can just pay me as I go along—only thing is, I don't know if I'll be able to get here early enough every day. I live in Bourbon."

The deal sounded good enough, but Bourbon, Indiana was seventy-five miles away. The commute to Portage was not a con-venient one for him.

"Mind if I talk to my wife a minute?" I asked.

"No problem."

Jeannine and I retreated to the kitchen and I told her that I felt he was a good man for the job. She then suggested that we put Sam up a couple of nights per week to reduce his travel time. I agreed.

I was willing to do anything to make her happy. So we offered Sam our couch and a place at our dinner table, and he agreed to begin work the next day.

When he left, I was hopeful. Jeannine seemed very happy, and we were getting more than we expected on the bathroom for less than we expected to pay—I still had five thousand dollars left and was already planning what piece of jewelry I could buy Jeannine or what cruise I could take her on to make her even happier. We actually slept together that night. I believed my marriage had a chance.

The first few days, I saw progress right away. When I came home from work, Sam would still be working and Jeannine would be making an elaborate, seven-course meal to feed him. I didn't mind because the entire family ate well and I figured she was just putting forth the extra effort to impress a guest. After dinner, Sam and Jeannine would venture to Lowes or Home Depot to pick out wallpaper, tile, bathroom fixtures and so on. I stayed home to watch the kids. They usually came back empty-handed and Jeannine claimed she could not decide. I also started to notice that I had less beer in the refrigerator, and new empty cans in the trash. Who was drinking my beer? My son? The handyman?

The end of October rolled around and I noticed there was barely any progress on the bathroom, with the exception of it being off-limits for use. In a house of eight—temporarily nine—people, this was a huge inconvenience. Sam's after-dinner trips to the store with Jeannine were stretching further into the night, until well after the stores closed. He had spent the last three consecutive nights at our house and was awake by the time I'd left for the commuter train at six in the morning. What was he doing all day? I was beginning to get suspicious.

I brought my concerns up to Jeannine in private. She exploded.

"Don't even accuse him of drinking your beer! You have no clue how much you drink! Sam's been under the house for the last few days, fixing something the original contractor did wrong. He can't go any further until he takes care of that."

"Calm down," I said, holding my hands up in surrender. "I was just saying—"

"Well don't!" she snapped. "Don't start criticizing things when you don't even know which end of the hammer to use. You're just looking for a reason to put him down because he's a handyman. He actually knows how to do something and you're nothing but a loser and a drunk!"

"No, really, I'm not. I was just concerned because it doesn't look like—"

"You have no idea how complex this project is. He could charge us so much extra for this, but he's not. Butt out and stop trying to insult him. I'll handle this and save us some money, too."

"I was just concerned because from an outside point of view, it looks like there's something going on between you two!"

If looks could kill, the one Jeannine gave me then would have been considered a weapon of mass destruction. "How dare you think that of me! The toll of the divorce is draining me. I have neither the interest nor the capacity to begin a relationship right now!"

As I watched her storm off, my heart sank. She still was determined to go through with the divorce.

The elated, excited, pleasant Jeannine was gone and her shark's teeth had returned. I didn't want to start yet another argument and jostle our already precarious situation, so I let it go, pushed all concerns aside and allowed her to handle things with the handyman. I hadn't had a drink for a while, so I went to a bar where no one would know me and proceeded to get drunk, but even that did not help my mood or alleviate my suspicions. In fact, it made them worse. I literally cried in my beer.

CHAPTER FOUR

To cope with what was happening and to try to understand how I could work to change things, I began to see a therapist in a sort of awkward, one-sided marriage counseling. I begged Jeannine to go with me, to help me work it all out, and she reluctantly went to one session in the beginning of November.

It did not go well. Not only did we argue the entire time, but anything that was said, she interpreted as something else I needed to work on, improve or change, and she was not willing to wait around for it. As far as she was concerned, she had done nothing wrong. She was already set on the divorce and nothing could change her mind.

By mid-November, the bathroom was not even halfway finished. Sam discovered that some rewiring needed to be done, so the job would take a lot longer than he had anticipated. Suspicions crept back into my mind, but since I did not want to accuse Jeannine and upset her again, I tried to convince myself that it was all my imagination. They say love is blind...I believe them.

The tension was so thick at home that for the sake of my children, I decided to take a friend up on his offer to stay at his condo in Chicago for some "time out." I would be minutes from work, and it would give both Jeannine and me some time to clear our heads and think everything through. Just maybe, she would miss me while I was gone. Maybe she would see how I helped out with the kids. Maybe she would realize that I was an essential part of her life and that she didn't want to give me up.

During that time, I told Sam that I was sorry, but he could not spend the night while I was not in the house.

"No problem," he replied. He agreed to make the daily commute, but warned me that he might not be able to make it every day. I had no issues with that. I just didn't want him to spend the night when I wasn't there. I figured since my older kids were still there, they would help me keep an eye on things.

I called Pete every day for updates. One day, sounding rushed and somewhat nervous, he blurted out, "Dad, I can't see much progress around here, and Sam stays until ten or eleven o'clock every night."

When I confronted Jeannine about why Sam was there so late, she told me that she had made arrangements for him to stay at a neighbor's house so he didn't have to make the long commute. I didn't like the idea, but what was I going to tell her? That he couldn't stay at a house that wasn't mine? A house I had no jurisdiction over? I let it go.

On December 13, 2003, one of Jeannine's friends called my cell phone while I was at work.

"Pat, just wanted to tell you…um…you should get home as soon as possible."

"Why? What happened? Is something wrong?"

"Well…" she said. "Look, I…you should just go home. See what's going on in front of your kids."

"What are you talking about? What happened to my kids?"

"Just…call Peter. He can tell you."

"You're not making any sense."

"I've got to go, Pat. Sorry."

Click.

I stared at my phone for half a minute, then took the rest of the day off. What was going on in front of my kids? Pete had been having his share of trouble with the law recently. They were minor

offenses, but offenses nonetheless—shoplifting, graffiti and van-
dalism—and Jeannine and I were at a loss for what to do. He
seemed to be struggling with himself, and we were never sure when
he was going to act up and be brought home by the police. Had he
done something in front of Mark, Barbara, Shannon, Mary and
Kristine?

When I got back to my friend's condo, I cracked a beer, then
called the house. My oldest son picked up the phone.

"Hello?"

"Hi, Pete."

"Hi, Dad." His voice was shaky, the way it used to get when
he was little and about to tell me something he knew I was not
going to be pleased to hear.

I told him about the phone call I had just received. "What's
going on, Pete?"

"I...I...um...well..." He took a deep breath. "So last night, I
woke up in the middle of the night, thirsty, and went to get a
drink. And I saw Mom on the couch...with Sam."

"*What?*" I shouted into the phone. "With Sam! With *Sam?*"

"Yeah. They were...well, you know."

"Is he there now?"

"Yeah."

"I'm on my way home."

"Dad, don't do anything crazy! Mom said she'd make my life
hell if I told you!"

"I'm on my way home. I'll be there soon."

I hung up the phone, slammed my beer and stormed out to my
car. How many nights had Sam spent there while I wasn't home? No
visible progress had been made on the bathroom, and now it made
sense. It was not a matter of what he was doing all day, but who.

I called up our next-door neighbor, Elaine, to see if she had
noticed his car there at night while I was away. She had. She even
told me that my children had mentioned that he was there all the
time, for every meal. I was livid. How could I have been so trusting?

So blind? Jeannine had scowled at me whenever I'd walked in the door, but she'd always had a smile reserved for Sam. No wonder she refused to budge on her desire to get a divorce.

While I had been stressing about work, my marriage, my life, I had been paying this man to have a joy ride on my wife.

I vented all of this to Elaine as I drove home like a maniac, speeding and cursing at people who drove safely.

"Calm down," she told me. "You really shouldn't barge in there. If you two get into some sort of altercation, he'll accuse you of attacking him—and you know Jeannine will side with him. You can't go to jail. Your kids need you."

"What am I supposed to do, Elaine? This man is screwing my wife!"

"Stop at the police station. Tell them what you just found out. This way if Sam attacks you, you have them there."

It was a good idea. I followed Elaine's advice and was glad I did. When the cops and I arrived at the house, Jeannine's car wasn't there. I went inside and found the bathroom door locked and Rolling Stones music blasting. I pounded on the door, with the two cops standing behind me.

"Open the door, Sam! Open the goddamn door!"

Sam emerged from the bathroom, looking rather clean for someone who was supposed to be doing hard labor, and he was wearing one of my shirts. A bottle of my Jack Daniels sat on top of his tool box. Having the police there was the only thing that prevented me from reaching back and letting him have it.

"Wearing my clothes, drinking my liquor, eating my food and screwing my wife! You motherfucker!"

Sam didn't look me in the eye. "What? No! I'm not—"

"My son caught you! Don't you lie to me, you bastard! Get the hell out of my house!"

An officer stepped between us. "All right. Enough." He turned to Sam. "Sir, I think it would be best if you grabbed your tools and left now."

"Get out of my clothes. I need to burn them," I said.

Sam nodded, but he still didn't look me in the face. He kept his eyes to the floor, like a dog that knew he had done something wrong.

As Sam was packing up his tools, Jeannine came home from picking Mary up from pre-school. I will never forget the look on her face as she walked in the house. Five police cars were out front and neighbors were already asking questions. She looked like a deer caught in headlights when she saw me. I guess the look on my face said it all.

I rounded on her. "Did you think I wouldn't find out?"

She had nothing to say for herself. She didn't speak a word to me.

The police escorted Sam off the property, and once they were sure Jeannine and I would not resort to violence, left us to battle it out. Jeannine packed Kristine, Mary and Shannon into the car and drove off. I didn't see or hear from her for four days. She did not pick up her cell phone. I had no idea where she was with my children. I called everyone I could think of and cried on their shoulders. I couldn't eat, I couldn't sleep and I couldn't stop drinking, either.

When she returned, I found out that she had taken the keys to my friend's condo where I was staying and went there, knowing I would not go back. She dropped the keys on the table and looked directly at me.

"I'm divorcing you. You're a filthy pig. Look at yourself. I'm so done with you! As far as I'm concerned, I'm single and I'll do as I please."

I could not believe how selfish she was! "How can you do this to me, Jeannine? This is the kind of message you want to send the kids?"

"You just don't understand!" she snapped. "We're in love. He's my soul mate and my one chance at happiness. I don't love you, Pat! And I want a divorce! If you really loved me, you'd want me to be happy, so go jump off a fucking bridge!"

CHAPTER FIVE

Just before Christmas of 2003, there was an unfortunate and sudden death in the family—Jeannine's seventeen-year-old niece, Leslie. At the time, I was still living in the Portage house, still sleeping on the couch and clinging to the naïve hope that this was a phase and we would pull through this bump in the road. By then, everyone in her family knew what was going on and had noticed a significant change in her attitude toward them.

I had to be the one to break the news to Jeannine. She was devastated, as was I. My heart went out to her family. I could not imagine the pain Jeannine's sister, Cassie, and her husband, Roger, were going through. To lose a child was the most tragic thing I could think of.

The wake was the day after Christmas. I went to work that morning and left early so I could make the services. When I arrived home, I saw Jeannine's car in the driveway, running, with the kids already inside, ready to go.

I stood there, confused for a moment, and then Jeannine came outside.

"Where are you going?" I asked.

"Leslie's wake," she answered smartly.

"Weren't you going to wait for me?"

"No. And I hope you don't go." She walked past me briskly, got in the car and before I could even say hello to my children, drove away.

She hoped I didn't go? How did she expect me not to want to pay my respects to my niece? I had known Leslie since birth, and over the last twenty years I had been a part of her family. It would be an insult to her memory and to her parents and siblings if I didn't show up.

I went inside to change and left only a half hour behind my family. When I arrived, the funeral home was jam-packed with relatives and friends who had come to say their last goodbyes. As I waited in a tremendously long line of mourners, I scanned the crowd for my children, but didn't see them anywhere. When I finally made it to the front to say some prayers and offer my condolences to Cassie and Roger, I asked if they had seen any of my kids. Jeannine's brother, Jerry, said that the kids were with his daughter, Jolene, but he had not seen Jeannine in some time.

"And Pat...I don't know what the little ones are wearing, but it's not really appropriate."

Dread filled me. What had Jeannine dressed them in? When I found Jolene and my kids, she, too, commented on their attire. Jeannine had put them in ill-fitting, soiled clothes and old sneakers; their hair was messy and dirty. I had no response. I was embarrassed. An hour later, I gathered up Shannon, Mary and Kristine and told the three older ones to let their mother know I was taking them home.

During the wake, Jerry tried to talk some sense into Jeannine. He pleaded with her to think of the kids, to keep in mind who fed them all and paid the mortgage, and to realize that if she committed financial suicide for the sake of her "soul mate," it would be her children who would suffer from it.

"You don't get it, do you?" Jeannine said calmly, a slight smile upon her lips. "I have a plan."

Jerry just shook his head and walked away.

The funeral was held the next day, and once again Jeannine made it clear that she did not want me to go.

"I'm leaving Mary and Kristine with you and taking Peter, Mark, Barbara and Shannon with me to Leslie's funeral."

"Don't you want to go as a family?" I asked.

"No. I do not want you there."

I was not about to miss the funeral, so I dressed Mary and Kristine and we went separately.

After the funeral, I politely declined an invitation to a family luncheon, so as not to make anyone uncomfortable. Instead, I brought Mary and Kristine home and put them to bed. Shannon, Barbara, Mark and Peter opted to stay with their cousins and mother.

At three o'clock a.m., I was pulled from sleep by a noise in the bathroom. I got out of bed and found Jeannine in there, using the sink to hold herself up to the mirror and admire her bare ass.

"What are you doing?" I asked.

Her head drooped a little as she swung it around to give me her usual look of disdain. She was drunk out of her mind.

"You drove like that with the kids in the car?" I asked her.

"Don't be stupid. I didn't drive. Mark did."

"Mark doesn't have a license!"

"Would you rather I had drove?"

"I'd rather you didn't get so shit-faced," I snapped. "Why were you out so late with the kids, anyway?"

"I got a new tattoo to honor Leslie's memory."

"On your ass?"

"Yes. On my ass." She pulled down her pants and said, "See?"

"Getting a tattoo took until three in the morning? I find that hard to believe. And I doubt they served liquor at the tattoo parlor."

"There was a bar next door. I had a few drinks while I was waiting for Pete and Mark."

I frowned. I loathed tattoos. "Peter got a tattoo for Leslie on his ass, too?"

"No. On his chest. He and Mark got matching ones."

"*What?* Mark is seventeen! You let him get a tattoo?"

"It's not a big deal."

"Not a big deal! What kind of mother lets her underage son get a tattoo?"

Jeannine ignored me and went back to examining her ass. "I can't wait to show this to Sam."

Fuming, I went back to bed, but my heart was racing and my blood was boiling.

Still concerned about Jeannine's behavior, her brothers, Jerry and Austin, along with Jerry's daughter, Jolene, drove from Chicago to Portage three days later to have a talk with her while I was at work.

Jolene, who had always been close with Jeannine, sat her down on the couch and tried to talk sense into her, pleading with her not to tear her family apart, to think of her children. She reminded Jeannine that she didn't work and had no desire to do so. Defensive and angry, Jeannine lashed out at Jolene with her usual song and dance. She wasn't happy, she deserved to be happy, Sam was her soul mate, she had a plan—though she would never reveal what, exactly, her "plan" was.

Jeannine leaped to her feet and Jerry and Austin each grabbed an arm. "I'm going to the bathroom!" she snapped. "Is that a crime in my own house?"

Jerry and Austin let go and Jeannine stomped upstairs. Jolene took the opportunity to go through Jeannine's purse and found several bottles of prescription drugs. When confronted, Jeannine snatched the pills out of Jolene's hand and told her it was none of her business, and asked them all to leave. They refused.

"Fine. Stay if you want. Stay the whole goddamn night!" She grabbed her coat and left the house, slamming the door behind her.

In the days that followed Leslie's funeral, despite her permanent memorial, Jeannine never once picked up the phone to call her grieving sister. She never took the time to go visit her, to bring her a comforting word or pray with her.

CHAPTER SIX

In January of 2004, I was laid off from my job again. Since I had been through this before, this time seemed trivial in comparison to the stress of the divorce. I was finally beginning to realize that Jeannine would never try to make our marriage work. And with everything that had happened since her announcement, I wasn't so sure I wanted to reconcile our differences anymore, either.

In the middle of the month, Jeannine asked if I would allow Sam to come back and finish the bathroom. He was going to bring along a friend of his, Jimmie Hackworth, to help him. Against my better judgment, I allowed it. I figured there was no hope for Jeannine and me, the bathroom needed to get finished, and since I wasn't working I could supervise and make sure they actually got the work done.

Sam arrived on Monday with his friend. Jimmie was in his early forties, but looked closer to sixty. He was short and stocky, with sleeves of tattoos up his arms. I could not help but notice the way he leered at Jeannine, watching her whenever she walked by, looking her up and down. I later learned that he had just gotten out of prison and needed the work, and that he and Sam had only known each other for a few months.

Sam and I had very little interaction. The air was cold between us. For the most part, I stayed clear of him while he was working, but when he and Jimmie took breaks, I checked on the bathroom. Some progress was actually being made, though it was obvious they were still taking their sweet time with it.

Friday came and it looked as if the bathroom would be complete by the end of the following week, so I gave Jeannine the go-ahead to pay them. On Monday morning, they didn't show up. It was the same on Tuesday. On Wednesday morning, I received a call from Ken, Sam's brother.

Apparently, that weekend Jimmie and Sam had gone out on an all-night drinking binge and ended up at Sam's trailer, where Sam had supposedly taken a shotgun and blown his brains out, right in front of Jimmie. I was in shock and speechless.

"I know this is awkward for you, Pat, given…well, given the circumstances," Ken told me. "But I just thought you should know."

"Yeah. Thank you. I'll let Jeannine know."

"Awkward" seems too tame a word to describe what it is like to have to break the news to your wife that her lover just committed suicide. I told her as gently as I could.

Jeannine was devastated. At first she just stood there, in complete and utter shock. "How could he do that?" she whispered, tears pouring down her face. "We were in love. We were soul mates. We had *plans*."

Jeannine dressed in all black to go to Sam's wake and funeral and sobbed on everyone's shoulders. She stood up front with his family and allowed people to believe she was his widow. The next day, in a tribute to his memory, she had his name tattooed on her ass, right beside the one dedicated to Leslie. Her ass was becoming a shrine for the dead.

She shut herself in the bedroom for days, burning candles and reading New Age spiritual books, using Sam's picture and memorial card that she had picked up at his wake as bookmarks. When she composed herself a little, she began to call the few friends she had left, begging them to come and console her. When they arrived, she threw herself into their arms, sobbing uncontrollably.

"Why? Why me? Why Sam? He was my love! My chance at being happy! He would never do this!" she wailed. "It must have

been that ex-con he was hanging around with! That bastard must
have killed him!"

She repeated the same story to Sam's family, who she didn't
even know, and to the police investigating the alleged suicide.

Our older children were in absolute shock. They couldn't
believe what they were witnessing—and neither could I. She did
not even get out of bed to make the kids breakfast or help them get
ready for school.

A week later, the phone rang. Still out of work and still taking
care of the kids while Jeannine pined away in her candlelit sanctu-
ary, I answered it.

"Hello?"

A somewhat familiar man's voice answered, "Can I talk to
Jeannine?"

"Who's calling?" I asked.

"Jimmie. Jimmie Hackworth."

"Hold on."

Part of me wondered if he was taking legal action against her
for slandering him. Another part worried that he was going to
threaten her. I went upstairs and knocked on the bedroom door.

"Jeannine?"

No answer. I knocked again.

"You have a phone call."

At first there was no answer, and then I heard her walking
toward the door. She opened it. Her eyes were red and bleary and
her hair was disheveled. She had a blanket wrapped around her and
a wad of tissues in her hand.

"Who is it?" she asked.

"It's Jimmie Hackworth," I said. I lowered my voice and
moved my hand over the mouthpiece. "Tell me what he says to
you, please? I don't want him threatening you or our kids."

Jeannine nodded and took the cordless phone from me, then
slammed the door in my face. I waited outside the door, but
couldn't hear anything. Twenty minutes later, she emerged from

the bedroom to get herself a new box of tissues from the hall closet.

"Well?" I asked.

"Well, what?"

"What did he want?"

"Oh. He just told me he had nothing to do with...with Sam's...d-death." She broke down into sobs again. When she composed herself, she continued. "He said they were just at his trailer drinking and doing a lot of drugs, when all of a sudden Sam grabbed the shotgun, and before Jimmie could stop him he blew his head off."

Before I could ask another question, she found her box of tissues and shut herself in her room again. I knocked, but there was no answer. I knocked again.

"Leave me alone," came the muffled reply.

I left Jeannine to her misery. I had to make the kids some lunch.

Jimmie called again the next day, and once again Jeannine took the call. She stayed on the phone with him for hours. They began to speak on a daily basis, talking about, according to Jeannine, Sam and how much they missed him. They leaned on each other, she claimed. Apparently, she had changed her mind about Jimmie's involvement in Sam's death.

I bumped into Sam's brother, Ken, one day while I was in Chicago looking for a job, so we grabbed a cup of coffee together. He told me that the autopsy had shown that there were eight kinds of drugs in Sam's body, including kitchen cleanser.

"I knew Sam really well—probably better than he knew himself sometimes. He only smoked pot—he was never into the bigger drugs. Something's not right. I mean, *kitchen cleanser*? I'm not alone in thinking his new ex-con friend had something to do with this. Sam didn't have his act together by any means, but he wasn't a big drug addict. So where did all these drugs come from? Jimmie, obviously."

"What was he in jail for, anyway?" I asked

"Sam said it was something about too many DUIs. But he was in prison for six years. I don't understand why it wasn't investigated further, if an ex-con, fresh out of jail, was the only witness."

I nodded. Anything was possible. I, too, found it an odd coincidence that all of a sudden Jimmie and Jeannine were the best of friends. It seemed to me that he was picking up where Sam had left off.

Jimmie even offered to finish the bathroom, free of charge. He couldn't commute, since he lived in Bourbon and had no driver's license due to his numerous DUI convictions, but he said that if Jeannine put him up in a motel for a few days, he could have the bathroom complete in no time. Jeannine agreed and the next thing I knew, she was picking Jimmie up every morning and driving him back every night. When I asked why it always took so long to drive him back to the motel, she told me they stopped for coffee and talked about Sam.

This pattern continued for a few weeks and Jeannine came home later and later each night. I suspected there was something going on between her and Jimmie and in the meantime, we, without any income, were paying for him to stay at a motel.

One day, I was downstairs when I heard Barbara scream. I dropped everything and rushed upstairs. I heard Jeannine shouting.

"What is the matter with you, Barbara? You can't just punch holes in the wall!"

"How could you? How could you?"

"You didn't see anything," I heard Jeannine shout. "You don't know what you're talking about."

"What's going on?" I asked as I reached the top of the steps. There was a small hole in the wall across from the upstairs bathroom, just the size of my little girl's fist. Barbara saw me and flung her arms around me. She pointed back at the open bathroom door, to Jeannine and Jimmie.

"He was kissing Mom! Make him leave, Dad. Make him get out of our house!"

"He was just hugging me! We were both upset!"

"He was kissing you!"

"No he wasn't! You're only thirteen. You don't know what you saw!"

"I do so!"

I believed my daughter. I calmly walked into the bathroom and quietly told Jimmie to gather up his tools and leave. Jeannine drove him back to the motel and didn't return for hours.

The following Thursday, Jeannine announced that she was going to spend the night at "a girlfriend's house out of town." She left that afternoon and didn't call until late Friday night to let us know she was going to spend another night at this mysterious girlfriend's house, and probably the weekend as well. "Probably," turned into definitely. We did not see or hear from Jeannine at all until she returned late Sunday night. We had no way of getting in touch with her and she didn't even call to check on the kids.

The following weekend, Jeannine went to visit another "out of town friend." Every weekend, and sometimes even during the week, she was gone. I knew very well what was going on, as did our three oldest children. I wanted to confront her, but I knew she would deny it. I had to submit evidence to her or catch her in the act, and I had bigger things to worry about.

CHAPTER SEVEN

It was now March of 2004 and I was still looking for work. Jeannine was absolutely no help and only spent money on her weekend getaways. It was our third month without income, we had no savings left, our mortgage was due on the fifteenth and we had six children to feed. I looked into various agencies to see if anyone offered help to families in our situation. The Red Cross offered a one-time donation of one hundred dollars. The local food pantry was open on Fridays. The Catholic food pantry was open the third Saturday of each month, and the county clerk's office offered to pay half of your mortgage if you put in thirty-two hours or more of community service each week throughout the month. We were desperate and had to do whatever it took. Jeannine, however, never lifted a finger to help out, so it was all up to me. But how on earth was I supposed to put in all that community service and find time to look for a steady job?

My son stepped up to the plate. Peter put in sixteen hours of community service per week in his mother's place so I could still look for a job three days a week. I was so proud of him. Together, along with the help of the church and the local food pantry, we were able to scrape by.

On Friday, March 19, Jeannine announced that she was going away, yet again, for the weekend. That Saturday was the Catholic Church's food pantry day for the whole month, but I had to leave early to go to the wedding of a niece on my side of the family. We desperately needed the Church's help, so I told Jeannine to make sure she got there before two o'clock p.m. She never went. Being with her boyfriend was more important to her than making sure her family had food on the table.

Jeannine spiraled down deeper into the twisted world she had created for herself. While the three older children understood what was going on, Shannon, Mary and Kristine were obviously confused. I can only imagine what was going through their little heads. *How could Mommy have a boyfriend when Daddy is still living with us? Why is Mommy always gone? Doesn't she love us anymore? Did we do something wrong?*

It was all about Jeannine. She was her own number-one priority and her kids were a distant second. Finally fed up with me being there, Jeannine called her lawyer to set a court date to have me removed from our home. He obliged, and the date was set for April 10, 2004.

I was actually looking forward to the April tenth court date. I was so fed up with Jeannine's bullshit that I was eager to show the courts just how much of an unreasonable woman she was. I had the utmost faith that the state of Indiana would take one look at this ridiculous woman and not only refuse to toss me out of my own house, but keep a close eye on Jeannine and her ex-con boyfriend.

The courts, however, disappointed me. When the judge came out, Jeannine's lawyer started rattling off her reasons for wanting me to vacate the house. When he finished, I waited for my lawyer to say or do something, but he remained silent.

"She can't do this," I whispered.

"Unfortunately," my lawyer whispered back, "since she filed for divorce, she has the upper hand."

I couldn't believe my ears. He was just going to sit there while I was ejected from my house?

The judge frowned and told me I had forty-eight hours to move out. I looked at my lawyer. He still said nothing. I stood up.

"Your Honor, may I address the court?"

He cocked an eyebrow. "You may."

"I believe my wife wants me to move out because she wants her boyfriend to move in. I don't want that ex-con there overnight with my kids."

He looked at Jeannine. "No overnight guests while the divorce is pending," he said. He banged his gavel. It was the end of the discussion.

I was numb. I had just been ejected from my own house. I had two days to pack my things and go—and my lawyer had done absolutely nothing. I was ordered to pay half of my income to Jeannine and she was supposed to prioritize her spending and maintain the house.

I went home and gathered up my clothes and whatever personal possessions I could fit in my car. I had no intention of taking anything from the house that Jeannine or the kids needed. It was their house, their memories. I was not about to take anything away from my kids.

When Jeannine came home, I once again asked her to reconsider the divorce. "You're committing financial suicide here," I said. "You can't hold on to the house by yourself—you've never really worked! Why don't you let me stay here with the kids and you can go on your merry way and do whatever you please?"

She clucked her tongue in exasperation. "I wouldn't leave the turtle with you and I won't lose the house. I'll work two jobs if I have to. I'll work at Déjà Vu if I need to!"

My jaw almost hit the floor. "A strip club? You're actually considering working at a strip club? Are you insane? What kind of example is that to set for the kids?"

"I'll do what I have to do. It's not your concern anymore."

Jeannine stormed off while I continued to pack. The forty-eight hours flew by and on Good Friday of 2004, I moved out of the house. That evening, Jeannine took off to Bourbon to be with Jimmie.

My brother and sister-in-law agreed to let me stay with them for a while. I was miserable. I don't even remember Easter Sunday. All I knew was that it was the first one in nearly twenty years that I had not spent with my kids. It was really depressing.

The following Monday, I started a temp job with a new company on the trading floor as a contractor. I was paid five thousand dollars per month, so I put aside twenty percent for taxes and figured Jeannine would get two thousand per month—more than enough for the mortgage, utilities and food.

I called often to check on my kids, to see how they were doing and how they were handling the whole situation. I found out that the same Monday I started my job, Jimmie was back in the house, supposedly to fix the bathroom. Pete told me that he had virtually moved in and while he occasionally tinkered around in the bathroom, for the most part, he putzed around the house and made himself at home while Jeannine doted on him. According to Pete, they smothered each other with affection to the point that it was a sickening sight to witness. When the little ones were asleep, Jeannine would drive Jimmie back to his motel and not return until the following morning—just in time to send Shannon off to school.

Pete's open dislike for Jimmie, as well as his daily reports to me, often led to screaming matches with his mother and her boyfriend. After two weeks of constant fighting, Jeannine walked in on Jimmie and Peter having yet another fight.

"You shouldn't be here! You don't belong in this house!" Pete screamed.

"Excuse me?" Jeannine interrupted.

"Mom, he shouldn't be here!"

"He is welcome here as long as I say he is. If you don't like it, tough."

"How can you do this? How can you live here and screw this guy when you yourself thought he killed the first guy you screwed around with? What is wrong with you? How do you think we feel about this? Do you think that we're stupid, Mom? Mark, Barbara, Shannon—even Mary and Kristine are confused!"

"That's *it*!" Jeannine said, slamming her fist against the wall. "How dare you question my decisions? Pack your bags and get out. *You* are the one who isn't welcome here anymore, Peter."

He was in shock. He moved his lips, but no sound came out. Finally, he said quietly, "You can't be serious, Mom."

"I am serious. I want you out of here by the end of the week. If you're so much of an adult that you can disrespect your own mother, you're enough of one to move out."

Peter gathered up his clothes and as many personal possessions as he could fit in his suitcase and duffel bag, then went over to our next-door neighbor Elaine's house. From there, he called me and told me what had happened.

I had been staying with my brother and sister-in-law since having been ejected from my house, but I could not ask them to take Pete in as well, so I thanked them for their hospitality and made different living arrangements. While I searched for an apartment for the next three months, Pete and I stayed in a hotel.

Shortly after Pete and I moved into the hotel room, he confessed to me that he was struggling with depression and that his mother's answer had always been to give him some of her pills. When he was high on these prescription drugs, he didn't think about anything and he felt "better." He'd begun feigning symptom after symptom so she would give him something. When she wouldn't give him anything, he would just take a few, since she left her pills out in the open. He, too, was becoming an addict, at the hands of his own mother.

His addiction was not simply broken by coming to live with me. Trouble still followed him around, and he was its eager companion.

CHAPTER EIGHT

The first month I spent out of the house was particularly brutal. I missed my kids. I was used to seeing them every day and I missed their laughter; I missed hearing their footsteps up and down the stairs. I even missed the sound of them fighting amongst themselves. I worried about Mark and Barbara and how they would handle the divorce. I worried about Shannon, Mary and Kristine. They must have been so confused. How do you explain such a bitter divorce to small children?

Rather than seeking therapy, Jeannine chose to tell them, "Mommy doesn't love Daddy anymore. Now we love Jimmie."

Now *we* love Jimmie. Words hold a lot of meaning for children. They take things very literally. Jeannine was basically instructing them to love her boyfriend of four months. It made all of the kids sick.

Barbara, a thirteen-year-old, redheaded, stubborn Irish girl, was absolutely disgusted by her mother's behavior and challenged Jeannine every step of the way. She thought that if she made Jeannine's and Jimmie's lives miserable enough, he would pack his bags and leave. She was sorely mistaken.

Why would Jimmie leave? Nine months prior, he had been living in a six-by-nine cell, eating prison food and counting down the days until he got out. Now he was practically living in a gorgeous, five-bedroom house, being fed home-cooked meals and sleeping with my beautiful wife. According to Barbara, Jeannine still drove him to the motel every night and didn't return until morning.

Desperate, I called my lawyer to see what could be done about it.

"Well, she's not doing anything illegal. From what you told me, he's not spending the night, so no one's going against any court orders. There's nothing you can do."

"Nothing?" I said. "There has to be something."

"I'm sorry, but these two are very clever about circumnavigating the law. If you bring them to court, they'll produce receipts from his stays at the motel and you'll just look like a jealous ex-husband—it won't work in your favor when the divorce is finalized."

I wanted to reach through the phone and strangle my lawyer with the cord. Didn't he understand that my children were in the house with a convicted felon? I took a deep breath to calm myself down.

"Look," I told him. "I have four young daughters in that house. One of them is thirteen and growing-up all too quickly into a beautiful young woman. Do you have daughters? Do you have any idea how terrified I am? My wife has known this man for four months and before she started sleeping with him, she accused him of murdering the other handyman she was screwing around with." I heard my voice get louder, but I couldn't control it. "She's on so many prescribed painkillers, I'm amazed she can feel a thing. She drinks every day, often heavily—she's not in her right mind! What if he tries something with one of my kids and Jeannine is too doped up to notice? Do you have any idea what he could do to one of my little girls? We need to do something!"

"I'm sorry, Pat, but there's nothing you can do."

"What if I just took my kids back to Illinois with me?"

"Then you would be charged with kidnapping and it wouldn't do you or your kids any good. You wouldn't see your kids for a long time."

I was torn. On the one hand, taking my kids across state lines and keeping them away from Jeannine would only temporarily pull them from harm's way. In the long run, I'd go to jail and wouldn't be able to see them. On the other hand, if I kidnapped my own children, it would bring attention to my situation and people would see what I was trying to do. Even if I went to jail, the kids might be taken away from Jeannine and her lover.

I decided to take my lawyer's advice: bite the bullet and pray for the best.

God help us, I thought.

Aside from Barbara's and Mark's reports, our next-door neighbor, Elaine, often kept an eye on things for me. Elaine was a responsible mother of three and had often tried to talk sense into Jeannine; the two had already had a falling out, but Elaine's daughter, Michelle, was Shannon's best friend.

Elaine was like a second mother to my kids. They were in and out of her house and yard all day long. She checked with them to see if they had been fed, kept an eye on them when they weren't being supervised—which was often—and invited them to stay the night at her house if any of them didn't feel right staying at home. My gratitude to her goes beyond what words can express.

Between Barbara and Elaine, I discovered that Jeannine and Jimmie were basically nocturnal. Like cockroaches, they scurried away at the first sign of light. At first, Jimmie kept a very low profile. It was almost as if he didn't want the neighbors to see him or know he was there. This all changed soon enough.

Near the middle of June, Jeannine asked her niece, Kelly, to come live with her and the kids. Kelly is a very sweet girl who I love dearly and have known since she was five years old. She has three kids of her own and wasn't getting along with her husband, so the house of seven turned into a house of eleven. Two of the very few friends Jeannine had left began to come over with their kids as well,

and soon the entire yard was filled with twenty to twenty-five people barbecuing, boozing and swapping pills. Thank God nothing
ever happened to the kids. I think that in the back of everyone's
mind, they knew Elaine was watching.

In June of 2004, Jeannine opened up an in-home day care—imagine! A woman who couldn't even be bothered to take care of her
own children opening up a day care! Jeannine's first and only clients
were a couple with a two-year-old boy and a six-month-old girl.

At that time, it often fell on little Shannon's shoulders to take
care of Mary and Kristine. She woke up with them, helped them
get dressed and ready, and did her best to make sure they were fed.
Since there was only so much an eight-year-old could do, Elaine
often took care of them. It wasn't her responsibility to look after
my kids, but she felt she had to—for their sake.

One morning, Shannon was playing with Michelle over at
Elaine's house, practicing cartwheels in her backyard. It was a
bright, clear June afternoon, not too hot—a perfect summer day.
As she hung freshly laundered sheets up on her clothesline, Elaine
peered over into Jeannine's backyard and shook her head.

Mary was running in circles around the above-ground pool,
barefoot, coming dangerously close to what looked like a broken
beer bottle near the filter. The little boy from the day care was
standing on the second rung of a ladder that was leaning against
the side of the house. The baby girl was in a carrier on top of the
picnic table, asleep in the sun. Mark and Barbara, being teenagers,
were seldom awake at that time of the morning, and Jeannine and
Jimmie were nowhere to be seen. Neither was Kristine.

Suddenly, Kristine appeared. She climbed up the pool ladder
and was walking along the edge of the pool—no inner tube, no
floatation device whatsoever, and no parental supervision.

"Kristine!" Elaine called. "Get down from there!"

Kristine looked up at the sound of her name, teetered a bit and
then regained her balance. She smiled at Elaine, giggled and waved.

Dropping her laundry back in the basket, Elaine turned toward Shannon. She knew Jeannine all too well. Even if she did help her out by saving Kristine from drowning, or that little boy from falling to his death, Jeannine would call the police if Elaine set foot in her yard. Or worse—forbid Shannon to spend the night or play with Michelle.

"Shannon," Elaine called. Shannon finished showing Michelle the one-handed cartwheel Barbara had taught her how to do and then looked up. "Get Kristine down from there—and that little boy. Tell your mother she needs to come outside and watch them."

Obediently, Shannon went into her own yard, told the little boy to get down from the ladder and coaxed Kristine down from the edge of the pool. When her sister's feet had been firmly set on the ground, Shannon told her, Mary and the little boy to stay away from the pool and the ladder and pointed out the pile of broken glass to them, and then moved the baby's carrier so she was more firmly in the shade. Shannon then disappeared inside the house and returned a few minutes later to Elaine's yard.

"My mom's still sleeping," she said as if it were the most natural thing in the world, then went back to practicing cartwheels and somersaults with Michelle.

Elaine shook her head, finished hanging her laundry and then spent the rest of the afternoon out back, keeping an eye on the children that Jeannine was supposed to be looking after. Finally, at around one-thirty p.m., Jeannine appeared, still in her pajamas.

As the summer progressed, the house in Portage became party central. Elaine called the cops on Jimmie because he lit a bonfire in the backyard and was fueling it with gasoline. On July Fourth, he was setting off fireworks while all the kids stood around. Elaine's son, who was sitting on his front step watching everything, was burned by a wayward whistler. When Elaine confronted Jimmie about it and asked him to stop before anyone else got hurt, he did not even apologize to her.

"Lighten up, lady," he said, exhaling his beer breath in her face. "It's the Fourth of July."

But it wasn't just the Fourth of July. Every day was a barbecue, there were always people over and there seemed to be plenty of food to go around—and expenses add up. Eventually, Jeannine maxed out her credit cards and could no longer afford to put Jimmie up at the motel. That's when he started staying over at the house.

When Barbara told me this, I called my lawyer, but he did nothing. I felt so helpless and frustrated, I didn't know what to do. It was bad enough that an ex-jailbird was there during the day, but now he was there while my children were asleep. It made my skin crawl.

I had to know more about him. I needed to make sure that his convictions were only DUIs and that there was absolutely no assault or molestation involved, so I looked up his criminal record online. There, I found the phone number for his parole officer.

I told him the situation and asked about Jimmie's criminal record, but his parole officer was more concerned about the house's location. As it turned out, Jimmie was not supposed to leave Marshall County without permission. Since Portage is in Porter County, he was in violation of his parole. I was so relieved. I thought this would get rid of him for good.

Elaine, too, took the time to call the parole officer to ask if she should be concerned about this man being around her kids. His response was, "He is not a nice man. Be careful."

When she asked him to elaborate on this, the parole officer told her he couldn't go into detail, but we could all read between the lines. Despite this, Jeannine began to spend the weekends and some weeknights with him in Bourbon, seventy-five miles from Portage, leaving our kids and the day care with Kelly, who was not licensed to run one. She made excuses for her absences, telling me that she was going to her sister's house, or to visit friends in Milwaukee, Wisconsin. When I called my lawyer to tell him this, again, he did nothing but tell me that they weren't really doing anything illegal.

The following Friday, Jeannine took Mary and Kristine and went to Jimmie's house in Bourbon, Indiana. She left Mark, Barbara and Shannon home with Kelly. By Wednesday, July 13, 2004—Mark's eighteenth birthday—Jeannine still had not returned. The court had allowed me visitation, so I drove out to Portage, picked up the kids and brought them out to dinner to celebrate Mark's birthday. I left notes at the house as to where we were, since we had no way of getting in touch with Jeannine. She never showed up. Seeing her boyfriend and having a good time were more important to her than her son's birthday.

Three Mondays in a row, Jeannine was still at Jimmie's house in Bourbon. Monday was garbage day. Imagine the pile of trash that accumulated from week after week of twenty to twenty-five people drinking and barbecuing in the backyard. There were thousands of flies, and the kids complained of mice in their rooms. In the sticky summer heat, the mountain of baking garbage gave off an odor that would have made sweat socks seem like sweet perfume.

Elaine called the health department. Jeannine was issued a citation and they sent a truck for special pick-up. Jeannine never forgot about garbage day again—she didn't want to risk bringing attention to what was going on in the house.

CHAPTER NINE

I stared at the letter in my hands and read it over again for probably the twentieth time. We were apparently six months behind on the mortgage.

If this is not addressed immediately, foreclosure proceedings will begin.

Foreclosure proceedings? Six months? What the hell was Jeannine *doing* with the money I sent her?

I called up the mortgage company and pressed about fifty numbers before I was put on hold for ten minutes, waiting to talk to an actual person. Finally, someone picked up.

"Thank you for holding. May I have your name and account number, please?" I gave the woman my name, account number, address, Social Security number, mother's maiden name, shoe size and whatever else she asked for, and then in a voice much too pleasant for what she had to do for a living, she asked, "And how can I help you today, Mr. Carroll?"

I explained the situation to her—that I had been court-ordered out of the home and Jeannine had been told to maintain it, which I thought meant paying the bills and the mortgage. I guess she thought differently.

The voice was no longer chipper and pleasant, but gravely serious. "I'm sorry, but unfortunately, since the mortgage is still under your name, you are in fact liable."

I took a deep breath and let out a shaky sigh. I could not believe this was happening. The woman from the mortgage company and I talked about our options, and I resolved to call Jeannine and give her an earful as soon as I got the chance.

Through various phone calls, I made sure that Jeannine's name was off every bill that was tied to me. In the process, I learned that she had also not been making her car payments, and that she had maxed out all of her credit cards to fund her backyard boozing barbecues.

I called my lawyer, but again, my pleas fell on deaf ears.

"It would take months to get into court," he told me. "By then, the house would be foreclosed and there would be nothing you could do about it."

I'm not a lawyer. I assumed that he was giving me good advice, that he had my best interests in mind. I took his advice and seethed.

By mid-November, the utility company had shut off all services to the house for non-payment. Without a word to neighbors, friends or me, Jeannine packed up the kids and whatever else she could and moved in with Jimmie, his sister and her husband.

It took me three days to find my kids, and it only happened because in a fit of frustration, I called one of Barbara's friends to ask about my daughter. To my surprise, I found out that Barbara had been staying there for the past few days.

Apparently, when Jeannine had told the kids to pack up and move in the middle of the night, Mark and Barbara had refused to go. They'd had enough. Mark was eighteen and in the middle of his senior year of high school, so he moved in with a friend on his own accord. Barbara, who was only thirteen and in the eighth grade, was originally told that she had to move, but she put up such a fight that finally Jeannine asked one of Barbara's friends' mothers if she would take her until Christmas break.

As soon as I located my kids, I made arrangements to transfer them to the schools by me. I thanked their friends' parents, but told them that Mark and Barbara's place was with me.

I felt horrible for the situation my children had been thrown into. One day, Shannon was going to school in Portage, and the next she was attending a grammar school in Bourbon. She never got the chance to say goodbye to her friends and classmates. She never even had the chance to tell her best friend, Michelle, that she was moving away. Mark was just about to graduate from high school. Barbara was just about to finish up middle school. And all of a sudden, they were moving to another city. Barbara cried for weeks.

After screaming at Jeannine and hearing no remorse on her part, we came up with an unofficial agreement that I would take care of the three older children, while she would care for the little ones. I wish I had battled her for them all, but her being a stay-at-home mom gave her an advantage that was almost impossible for me to overcome. In Indiana, a no-fault state, the courts would not allow me custody unless Jeannine agreed. Of course, she wasn't about to relent.

My three youngest children were now living a hundred and twenty miles away from me, in another state. Under the previous arrangement, I had some additional parenting time on Wednesday evenings, but now I had to forfeit that. It just wasn't feasible on a work night.

On my parenting weekends, Jeannine and I met at a halfway point, but this ended up being a three-hour ordeal for me, what with the Chicago rush-hour traffic. To make matters worse, I didn't know any of Jeannine's new neighbors, so I had no one to check on things for me, no one to report back to me if something was amiss. Then I found out from Barbara that Shannon, Mary and Kristine were not supposed to tell me anything that happened at Mom's because "Dad will make trouble." Their house was like Las Vegas: what happened there, stayed there.

CHAPTER TEN

In our mediation session the previous August, Jeannine and I had agreed to alternate holidays with the kids. Jeannine had them that first Christmas, so I drove Pete, Mark and Barbara to the halfway point on Christmas Eve. They were excited during the car ride over. Though they disapproved of their mother's behavior, they still loved her, missed her and were looking forward to spending Christmas with her. They greeted Jeannine with hugs and kisses, said goodbye and Merry Christmas to me, and then got in Jeannine's car. We went our separate ways and I couldn't help but feel a pang of loss. It was Christmas, and I wouldn't see my children's delighted faces in the morning.

The entire drive back to Oak Lawn, I thought of Christmases that had gone by, pictured the kids' looks of awe and delight when they had come downstairs and seen the presents under the tree. I spent Christmas Eve alone, already planning out next Christmas in my head—what I wanted to do for them, activities for the little ones, cookie-baking with the older ones. It was all I could do for now.

Christmas morning, I woke up bright and early, half expecting to feel the kids jumping on my stomach and telling me to wake up so they could open presents. But there was no Shannon, no Mary or Kristine, not even Barbara, Mark or Pete. I rolled over and went back to sleep, only to be awakened by the phone's ringing.

"Hello?" I said, the grogginess still apparent in my voice.

"Dad?"

Barbara's voice was cracking. She was crying. At once I was awake, alert and ready.

"Honey, what's wrong?"

"Can you come get us?"

"Come get you? Why? What happened?"

"Please, just come get us. We don't want to be here anymore." She sniffed and sobbed for a few seconds, then continued, "Mom and Jimmie are disgusting. They're hanging all over each other, and this morning Jimmie woke up and asked Mom to take a shower with him and she *did!* And when—when she came out, Mark, Peter and I told her that they were both sickening, and she just told us it was to save time and that we should get over it! But she took long enough showering with him and the bathroom's not sound-proof! It was gross!"

"Sweetheart, I can't come and get you unless your mother gives the okay. She—"

"Dad, she doesn't care how uncomfortable it makes us. We just want to go home. Please come get us. Please..." Barbara broke down into sobs. "Dad, please..."

"Put your mother on the phone."

Barbara handed the phone to her mother.

"Yes?" Jeannine said, the annoyance apparent in her voice.

"Barbara says the kids want to leave."

"Merry Christmas to you, too, Pat."

I ignored her. "Are you okay with the kids leaving? Barbara is begging me to pick them up."

Jeannine clucked her tongue. "Fine," she said. "But I'm not driving them anywhere. I've got enough to do today."

So on Christmas Day, 2004, I drove back to Bourbon, Indiana, and picked up all six of my children. I was driving a Buick Park Avenue—a big enough car, but it had only six seatbelts, and including myself, we needed a total of seven.

So, Mary and Kristine had their car seats in the back, and Mark wedged in between them and belted in; Peter and Barbara sat in the front with me, and that took up the rest. Shannon, with no room left, voluntarily squeezed herself into an empty spot on the floor between the front and back seats. We were like clowns stuffing ourselves in for a circus performance. It was a long ride back to Oak Lawn, Illinois, but I hoped that it would go fast and that nobody would be too uncomfortable in the meantime.

But before we even really got going, we had to stop. As soon as we hit highway thirty, a police car pulled up behind us, lights flashing; as I pulled over slowly, I told all the kids to make sure they had their seatbelts on tight—and then remembered Shannon down there on the floor.

Without even thinking, we all threw our winter coats on top of her, making her all but invisible. As the cop approached the car and asked for my license and registration, I prayed that he wouldn't get too curious about the pile.

The whole thing took maybe ten minutes; after running a check of my license, he found no reason to hold me there and so he let me and the kids just drive off. Shannon had been so still the whole time, the officer hadn't suspected a thing—though she did take a few deep, grateful breaths of fresh air once Mark pulled all the coats off of her.

Later, I found out that this ambush had not been a coincidence. It was a couple of weeks after it happened, when I went to meet Jeannine and get the kids at our regular pick-up spot. Carla, Jimmie's sister, was there when I arrived and in her usual classless fashion, had a bunch of really nice things to say to me. One of them was a story about how on Christmas, she had waited until I'd picked up the kids and then phoned the local police station, telling them that she'd seen a guy in a burgundy Park Avenue driving along with a bunch of children who were not wearing seatbelts. This was so vindictive, so petty, that I almost couldn't believe it when I heard it. But then, I remembered the source.

Hours later, we arrived safe and sound at my apartment in Oak Lawn, Illinois—and in relatively good spirits as well. I had been planning on having leftover macaroni and cheese for my solitary Christmas dinner and had no idea what we were all going to eat, but when we got to the apartment, the kids helped me pull out whatever I had in the cabinets and refrigerator—canned soup, peanut butter and jelly sandwiches, even the mac and cheese. We cooked it all up and devoured it like it was the best holiday spread on earth. We were just happy to be together; nothing else seemed to matter.

I had bought a tiny Christmas tree that year, just the right size for my small apartment, but had splurged on literally a ton of gifts for the kids, and they spent what seemed like hours opening them all. The happiness we shared on that day was just what I'd needed, and I was so very grateful that we had the chance to enjoy Christmas Day together.

Over the course of the next few months, I had very little knowledge of what went on while my little ones were at home in Bourbon. I didn't have Elaine there to keep an eye on them, and they didn't want to upset their mother, so they didn't tell me anything that happened in their lives.

Time went on as usual. Barbara finished middle school and began to make some new friends. Mark joined the track team and graduated from high school in Illinois. Over the summer, I had the kids every other week. Mark got a job and Barbara would watch her little sisters until I came home at four p.m. On the weekends, we were out of the house from ten a.m. until dark.

My sister-in-law, Sara, called me "Disneyland Dad." I kept telling myself that I was just trying to make the most of my time with the kids, but part of me, I think, was trying to compensate for all the adversity in their lives. They were growing up in poverty because their mother was going through a mid-life crisis and couldn't manage her finances. I wanted to give them as normal a life as possible.

CHAPTER ELEVEN

At 9:30 p.m. on October 7, 2006, my phone rang. I checked the caller ID a half second before snatching it from the receiver, but I already knew it would be Jeannine, my soon-to-be ex-wife.

"How's Shannon doing?" I asked. Our ten-year-old daughter was in the hospital, sick with some sort of stomach virus.

"Not good," Jeannine said. "They still can't figure it out, but they said it's not a stomach flu. They think it's something more serious."

My heart began to race.

No. Not my Shannon.

"Serious? How serious? Like cancer?"

"No. At least the doctors here don't think so. She's being transferred in a few minutes to Riley Children's Hospital in Indianapolis."

My mouth went completely dry and my still-fluttering heart fell to my stomach. Transferred? What was so wrong with my Shannon that the doctors at St. Joseph's couldn't figure out what the problem was? Riley's was a great hospital, don't get me wrong—it's a McDonald's-sponsored facility, every doctor on staff is a specialist, everything state of the art—but the fact that my daughter's condition was so serious that she had to be sent there... Well, that was not a good sign. I tried my best not to panic.

"Is she there? Can I talk to her?"

"Pat, her tongue's all swollen—"

"I know," I said, a little more sharply than I meant to. I paused, and then continued in an even tone. "Can I please just talk to Shannon?"

"Hang on." I waited a few seconds, then heard Jeannine's voice again, distant this time. "It's Daddy."

When I heard Shannon's voice on the other end, I could barely understand what she was saying. She said hello, but mostly grunted to answer yes or no questions. I didn't want to keep her on the phone. I could tell it hurt her to talk, so I kept the conversation brief.

"I'll be there as soon as I can, okay, honey?"

"Uh-huh."

"I love you."

She moaned something in return, probably telling me she loved me, too. I said goodbye, then hung up the phone, grabbed my car keys and ran out the door.

Screaming down the highway, doing at least eight-five miles per hour, I tasted bile in the back of my throat and fought down the queasiness in my stomach. *Something serious*, Jeannine had said. I tried to tell myself that this was just her overreacting again, pulling our children into her hypochondriac world of obscure ailments, but my conscience wouldn't let me. No father could ever brush aside concerns if there was the slightest possibility that one of his children could be in danger. Besides, doctors were concerned as well—concerned enough to transfer Shannon to Riley Children's Hospital.

I thought back to the previous weekend when I'd had Shannon with me and couldn't remember any real signs of illness. I'd picked up her and the other girls on Friday night and taken them to a drive-in movie. The next day, we went to a Holiday Inn where we decided to stay overnight so we could swim in the pool. Shannon was in the water most of the day on Saturday, and that night, started saying that her arm hurt. I gave her an aspirin, but on Sunday morning she was still complaining of pain.

Mark took his sisters home that night and aside from what we figured was a pulled muscle from too much swimming, Shannon seemed okay. She went to school on Monday, and that was when she'd started saying that she didn't feel good. On Tuesday, she'd thrown up in school. Assuming it was just a stomach virus, Jeannine had brought her to the pediatrician the next day. He'd prescribed for Shannon some antibiotics and ordered bed rest and plenty of fluids. By Friday, she still couldn't keep anything down and was having trouble swallowing, so Jeannine had called to tell me that she was bringing her to the emergency room.

I panicked, ready to jump in the car and make the long haul from Oak Lawn, Illinois, to Plymouth, Indiana. Jeannine had talked me out of it, telling me not to take the three-hour trek for a stomach flu. She had said that she would keep me posted.

She had kept her promise and updated me a few hours later. They were going to monitor Shannon for twenty-four hours and give a diagnosis then.

I'd tried calling Jeannine several times during the day to check on the situation, but her phone had been turned off while she was in the emergency room with Shannon. When I'd finally received the phone call I had been waiting for all day, I truly expected Jeannine to tell me my little girl was doing much better—that the doctors had said she would recover in a few days—not that she was being transferred because the doctors thought it was "serious."

My head was swimming as I weaved in and out of traffic, cutting other cars off if they threatened to slow me down. Streetlights, headlights and taillights whipped by me in a blur of red and white. Other cars were not vessels carrying other people, but objects blocking my path to my daughter.

By a stroke of luck, I missed every cop on the road that night and made it to Indianapolis by midnight.

I burst in through the doors of Riley Children's Hospital's Intensive Care Unit. I looked back and forth for a second or two, and then leaned over the nurses' desk.

"Excuse me, I'm looking for Shannon Carroll."

She nodded to her left. "Cubicle four." I followed her gaze and saw Jeannine standing outside one of the cubicle doors—with Jimmie, her jackass, ex-felon, drug-addict boyfriend, whose sole purpose in life seemed to be to get under my skin.

I thanked the nurse over my shoulder and half-jogged to Shannon's cubicle, nearly knocking over another nurse in the process. Ignoring Jeannine, I rushed past her to go see my daughter. Jimmie, who was wearing a dirty t-shirt and stained jeans, stood in front of the door to block my way.

"You can't go in there," he said, holding his arms out to either side.

"The hell I can't! I'm her father!"

I pushed past the dummy and entered the cubicle. Shannon was lying on the bed, looking frightened, tired and thoroughly miserable. IVs hung from posts on her bed and various monitors blinked with readings I didn't understand. Her tongue was so swollen that she had to keep her lips slightly parted, and her eyes were red—she had been crying. When she looked up and saw me, the tiniest bit of relief flashed over her face.

"Hi, sweetheart," I said, leaning over to kiss her forehead. Her skin burned with a fever. Shannon grunted in response.

There was a young, red-haired nurse in there with her, prepping a needle to draw some blood. I introduced myself.

"I'm Kate," said the nurse. She smiled—that practiced, soothing smile of one used to calming hysterical families—and filled me in. "We're just going to run some blood tests. Dr. Costello has a few ideas. He should be around shortly to meet with you and answer any questions."

"Thank you." I turned back to Shannon and stroked her hair. It was stringy and wet with perspiration. I wanted to talk to her, to ask her questions and get her mind off things, but she was having so much trouble talking that it would only serve as a reminder. "You're going to be okay, sweetheart. The doctors here are going to help you out."

"She's been pretty brave so far. Little pinch," said Nurse Kate as she pressed the needle into Shannon's arm. "Right, Shannon? One of my bravest patients."

Just as the nurse finished, the doctor arrived. He was friendly looking with a neatly trimmed beard and glasses, and I guessed him to be in his late forties. He said hello to Shannon, and then introduced himself to me. He spoke in a brisk, professional manner, but his voice carried soothing tones. I immediately felt better that this was the man taking care of my little girl.

"I'm Dr. Costello. I specialize in infectious diseases."

"Pat Carroll. I'm Shannon's dad."

He shook my hand—a good, firm handshake. I felt a little better. This was a man confident in his abilities. "Mr. Carroll, I'm just going to do a quick exam on her, then would you mind meeting with me? I have a few questions about Shannon."

I agreed, kissed Shannon's forehead again and then went outside, where Jeannine and Jimmie were waiting.

"Told you you couldn't go in there," he said when I appeared.

"The doctor was fine with me being there," I snapped. The last thing I needed was Jerko's comments.

A few minutes later, Dr. Costello appeared with a clipboard. His expression was impossible to read. The knot in my stomach tightened.

The usual pleasantries were exchanged and the questioning began—starting with me.

"What's wrong with Shannon?" I asked. "Why is her tongue swollen like that?"

"I have a few ideas," the doctor said. "I just have a few questions for you three that might help clarify things. Was there recently any construction in the neighborhood?"

There was none going on in mine. I turned to Jeannine. She shook her head.

"What about in nearby parks or baseball fields—anywhere she played?"

Again, the answer was no.

Did she swim in any ponds? Did she complain of any mosquito bites? Had she been bitten or scratched by any wild animals? Did either Jeannine or I own a cat that was permitted outside? No, no, no and no.

With each successive question, Dr. Costello's mouth tightened into a thin line and there was a deeper furrow to his brow. Our answers were not helping him.

Finally, he glanced over his clipboard and said, "Well, we're going to do some blood tests and spinal taps. I think it might be West Nile."

Jeannine let out a wail and buried her face in the big jerk's chest. I felt as if all the blood had been drained from me. *West Nile.* I didn't know much about the disease, but from what I understood, neither did most doctors.

"Did we catch it early on?" I asked.

"I'm not even sure if it is West Nile, but I won't know how far it has progressed until the test results return."

I asked him for specifics regarding West Nile, confessing that all I knew about it was that it was dangerous and transmitted by mosquito bites. He briefed me on the disease, how it affected the nervous system and how the symptoms varied from mild to extreme. Like all doctors, when he explained things in the simplest terms he knew, the explanation only left me with more questions. He had other patients to see, but he did promise to gather some literature from the Internet for me to look over when he returned.

"I've given Shannon a mild sedative to help her sleep. You should try to sleep, too. There's a private waiting room the nurse will show you to."

Dr. Costello left to tend to his other patients, and Nurse Kate led us out of the ICU and down the hall. The private room was cold, windowless, and all around the perimeter were chairs and sofas—barely adequate for sitting, and very uncomfortable for sleeping. In the center of the room was a bare coffee table and between two chairs was an end table piled with outdated magazines. A TV hung in the corner adjacent to the door.

"Let me get some pillows and blankets for you," the nurse said. She disappeared down the hall.

Still sobbing and leaning on Jimmie, Jeannine entered the room first and sat down on one of the sofas. Jimmie sat by her side, arms around her, whispering something. Then, he looked up at me and flipped me the bird.

I ignored him, fuming at his lack of maturity in such a horrible situation. I sat down on one of the chairs and stared at the blank screen of the TV, shaking my leg with impatience. I could feel his eyes on me, staring me down, trying to get me to look in his direction again. Since I'd met him, he had liked to get a rise out of me. This time, I refused to give the jerk the satisfaction.

It bothered me to no end that this man was partially responsible for the welfare of my three youngest children. I barely trusted Jeannine to take care of Shannon, Mary and Kristine, what with her tendency to distort the truth to boost her own image and her methadone addiction—which I suspected her lover shared. While the medication was prescribed to her, she abused it, and I believe she was constantly faking pain to have her dosage increased.

"Jeannine," I said. "Where are Mary and Kristine?"

"I left them with a neighbor—Tammy."

"Can I have an address and phone number?"

"Can we not talk about this now? I'll get it to you later."

I dropped it for the time being. We were all worried about Shannon, though I seriously doubt that Jimmie really cared.

Nurse Kate returned with some blankets and pillows for us; she placed them on the coffee table and then left again in a hurry. I pulled my cell phone out of my pocket and looked down at it. No reception.

I pulled my coat tighter around me. It was cold, as only hospitals and jails could be—that bone-chilling chilliness stemming more from the fear of what could happen next than the actual temperature. The hospital's thermostat could have been set at eighty degrees and I still would have shivered.

Why was this happening? Shannon was such a good kid—bright, active, beautiful, always helping out with her younger sisters. It wasn't fair. She didn't deserve this.

I searched my brain for any memory that would help figure this out. I had been fortunate enough to have my children for a good part of the summer and we'd been out and about most of the time—so often, in fact, that we'd eaten at Denny's, or Shannon's favorite, Taco Bell, more often than we'd eaten at home. Had there been construction near any of the places we'd gone? Not that I could recall. I didn't remember Shannon complaining of mosquito bites at all during the summer, either. Had there been any animal scratches or bites?

No, I thought. *If Shannon had been bitten or scratched, I'd have taken her to the emergency room then and there.*

I glanced over at the jerk and Jeannine. He gave me the finger again. I sighed, stood up, grabbed a blanket from the coffee table and headed out the door.

"Where the hell are you going?" the jerk asked.

I just ignored him and continued down the hall. It didn't feel right sitting in that waiting room with those two. Shannon may have been sleeping, but I was going to be there by her side whenever I could.

I went down to cubicle four and slowly opened the door. Shannon was lying on her back, head lolled to one side, fast asleep. I closed the door as quietly as I could and sat down in the plastic chair next to her bed. Draping the blanket over myself, I tried to find a comfortable way to sit, but in the end I found I wasn't tired at all. I was terrified.

The cubicle was even colder than the waiting room. Careful not to wake her, I made sure Shannon was tucked in. She seemed warm enough and barely stirred as I pressed the blanket around her.

By the dim green light of the monitors, I watched Shannon sleep. I nodded off a few times during the night, but never for long. The slightest sound jolted me awake and I began to worry all over again. My neck was stiff and my back was sore, but it didn't matter. The important thing was, when morning came and Shannon woke up in unfamiliar surroundings, still in pain, she looked over and saw her dad sitting there.

"Good morning, sweetheart," I said when she looked over at me.

Shannon smiled as best she could, but said nothing. It was getting harder for her to talk.

A nurse came in shortly afterwards, making rounds. She introduced herself to me and to Shannon—her name was Emily—and chattered pleasantly as she checked the IVs, taking both of our minds off things for a little while.

"When will Dr. Costello be in?" I asked.

"He's already here," the nurse said. "I don't think he knew you were, though. I think he thought you were out with Shannon's mother and stepfather."

"Shannon's what?"

The nurse hesitated. "Mother and stepfather."

"He's not her stepfather. He's just her mother's latest fling." I could not keep the bite out of my voice.

The nurse nodded. "Sorry about that. At any rate, the test results are in. Like I said, I don't think he knew you were still here, so I'll let him know."

Where the hell had Jeannine gone? Her daughter was in the hospital and she was off God knew where?

And the nerve of that jackass, calling himself her stepfather! I thought. It made my blood boil to learn that that ex-felon had claimed kinship to *my* little girl. It was bad enough that Jeannine had tossed our marriage away for that loser—though technically, she had tossed it away for *another* loser: Sam. She had always been quirky and irresponsible at best; it was only recently that she had gone off the deep end.

CHAPTER TWELVE

The results came back negative for West Nile. The flood of relief quickly receded, however, as Shannon's condition worsened and no one knew how to treat her. By Monday, we still had no idea what was wrong with her. I was exhausted, dirty and without an appetite. Coffee became my staple. The nurses, doctors, orderlies and cafeteria workers all knew me by name. My back ached from sleeping in uncomfortable chairs, but I just couldn't leave Shannon's side.

Jeannine and the jerk made their rounds at the hospital, and they stayed at the nearby Ronald McDonald House. Jimmie continued to make my life difficult, staring me down and then shooting me the finger if I looked his way, standing in my path, refusing to move until I made eye contact with him so he could make some smartass comment.

While Shannon slept one night, I went to get myself another cup of coffee. Past the nurses' desk and out of the PICU (Pediatric Intensive Care Unit), I had to walk past the waiting room to get to the elevator. From the corner of my eye, I saw Jeannine and the jerk sitting on the couch, watching TV.

Seconds after I walked by, I heard sneakers squeaking behind me. I picked up my pace. When I reached the elevator, my timing was perfect—it opened just as I approached. A nurse stepped out and I stepped in.

"Hold the elevator!" Jimmie called out. Having no desire to stand next to him for even ten seconds, I hit the "close doors" button. Just before they closed, his hand pushed between them, causing the doors to spread back open. I ground my teeth.

He stepped into the elevator, keeping his hand on the side of the doorway to prevent the doors from closing. He peeked out into the hallway.

"Do you mind?" I asked. I was in no mood for his stupid games today.

"Jeannine's coming."

Sure enough, I heard the steady click of Jeannine's heels on the hallway tile. She was in no rush.

"Forget it!" I snapped. "I'll take the stairs!"

Shoving past him, I stomped out of the elevator and down the hall. The nurse who had come out of the elevator watched as I threw open the door to the stairwell and slammed it behind me. I went straight to the cafeteria, grabbed my coffee and took the stairs back up. Jeannine and Jimmie were milling around the gift shop.

By the time I made it back to the PICU, I was still fuming. Every member of the hospital personnel could feel the tension in the air. I was irritable; I was trying to be civil for Shannon's sake, but that man infuriated me. He seemed more concerned with getting under my skin than with Shannon's well-being. Already stressed, with the jerk there, I was a ticking time bomb. Who knew when I would explode?

Jeannine and Jimmie returned, arms laden with a huge arrangement of flowers and yet another teddy bear to brighten up Shannon's room. I could feel the muscles in my neck start to tighten. One of the nurses stepped in front of them and said something quietly.

"You're kidding me, right?" Jimmie said, loud enough for the entire PICU to hear.

"I'm sorry, sir. The PICU is for family only and we think it would be best if you waited outside. The tension is not good for any of our patients," the nurse said, raising her voice a little. She was a small woman, but she projected the aura of one not to be trifled with; she spoke in polite tones, but something in her voice said that she would not be polite for long. Even the moron must have sensed it—he didn't argue. As he left the PICU, I felt the knot in my chest loosen. *One less thing to worry about*, I thought.

Jimmie tried to sneak in later that day, but was stopped and asked to leave the hospital altogether. With him gone, I could concentrate on worrying about Shannon.

"Is there a member of the Carroll family here?" one of the nurses at the PICU desk called.

Half-asleep in the chair next to Shannon's bed, I heard my name and lifted my head. The nurse repeated herself. I stood up, rubbing the back of my neck and clearing the sleep out of my throat.

"Did you say, 'Carroll'?" I asked, poking my head out of the cubicle.

"Yes," she said, holding up the handset of the desk phone. "You have a call."

Jeannine and I had received several calls over the course of the past few days, mostly from family members concerned about Shannon, asking how she was doing and when visiting hours were. Thanking the nurse, I grabbed the phone and took a deep breath, bracing myself to give whoever it was a summary of events. I wanted to sound hopeful, but despair was beginning to creep in after four days of not knowing anything while Shannon's condition worsened.

To my surprise, it was one of the nurses from Shannon's pediatrician's office.

"Good morning," I said after she had introduced herself.

"Mr. Carroll, I received a call from a woman named Tammy, asking about Shannon."

"Oh yes. She's a neighbor." That was all I knew about her: she lived down the street from Jeannine in Bourbon, Indiana. I had never met her, but she was looking after Mary and Kristine while Jeannine and I were in the hospital with Shannon.

"She said that over the summer Shannon was bitten by a bat and was wondering if that had anything to do with her illness."

"She *what?*"

The nurse repeated what Tammy had told her, and I was absolutely stunned. I thanked her and quickly hung up the phone. Leaning over the desk to the nurse who had told me about the call, I asked, "Could you please have Dr. Costello paged?"

The next few minutes were a blur. My hands were shaking. *A bat*, I thought. *A goddamn bat.* It hadn't happened while she was with me, and Shannon had never said anything about it. Why hadn't she said anything to me?

I fumbled with my cell phone, cursing out loud every time I pressed the wrong button, going through the address book to find Jeannine's number. I heard Dr. Costello's name being called over the hospital's PA system. When I finally found Jeannine's number, I had no reception, so I darted toward the doors to go into the hallway—where I nearly ran Jeannine over.

"There you are. There's news about Shannon," I said.

"What? Do they know what's wrong?"

"Maybe. Did Shannon say anything about—" I stopped as I spotted Dr. Costello in the hall, heading our way. I rushed out to meet him. "I just got a call," I said. "A neighbor said that over the summer Shannon was bitten by a bat."

Jeannine let out a little gasp and pulled her hands to her lips. Her gaunt face was chalk white. Pulling her fingertips away from her mouth, she whispered, "I forgot about that."

My head snapped in her direction. I felt as if it were about to explode with rage.

"I'm going to order some more tests," Dr. Costello said, hurrying into the PICU.

"You *forgot*? Are you fucking *kidding* me, Jeannine? How could you forget something like this?"

Teary-eyed, Jeannine shook her head. "I just did. I forgot."

"You were *asked* if she was bitten by any animals! Didn't you even think about the question? Didn't you bring her to the hospital when it *happened*?"

"Oh, my baby!" Jeannine wailed.

"Don't even start with that! You knew about this and for four days kept quiet!"

"I told you! I forgot!"

"Shannon's been in this state for four days and you only tell us *now* that this happened? What if Tammy had never called? Shannon could have died!"

"I *forgot*, Pat! It *happens* sometimes!"

Our noses were inches from each other, but we were both shouting at the top of our lungs. Jeannine's face was no longer white, but purple with rage, as I was sure mine was.

Nurses came flooding out into the hallway, trying to calm the both of us down. I shook them off.

"How could you be so irresponsible? This is our *daughter*! If it was you, you'd have been in the hospital that night! What possessed you to ignore it?"

"I put peroxide on it! I thought it'd be fine!" Jeannine said.

"You understand that Shannon could have rabies? *Rabies!* Who the hell gets rabies in this day and age?" I yelled.

"Mr. Carroll, if you do not keep your voice down and calm down, I will have to ask you to leave the hospital!" One of the nurses stepped between Jeannine and me, her hands planted firmly on her hips. It was the same nurse who had tossed Jimmie out.

I had to be near Shannon. I was not about to let myself be ejected from the hospital—especially if that opened the possibility for the moron to return.

"I'm going for a walk," I said, turning on my heel and marching down the hall.

I wanted to strangle Jeannine. I wanted to shake her until every forgotten memory spilled out. How do you forget something like that? How do you ignore it in the first place? What was she waiting for? Didn't she even *try* to remember anything that could have caused this? Or was she too busy deciding which bouquet of flowers to buy Shannon next? Was she covering something up? How could she possibly have a reasonable excuse for this? My mind was racing with unanswered questions.

I didn't storm around the third floor for very long. I wanted to be there when Dr. Costello returned with the test results. Still angry, but a little more in control of myself, I returned to the PICU, refusing to even look at Jeannine. Dr. Costello saw me approaching and looked at me with his impassive eyes.

"Well, it looks like Shannon has rabies. From what I've learned, the bite was back in June, so she's very far along with this and at terrible risk."

My heart felt as if it had been dunked into a tub of ice. I glared at Jeannine. *Since June.* My little Shannon was lying in a hospital bed, miserable, in pain and fighting for her life because her incompetent mother had let this go since June!

"There was another girl in Wisconsin who survived a case of rabies this bad," Dr. Costello continued, "named Jeanna Giese. I placed a call to the doctors there to get the protocol. They should be calling me back in a few minutes. Now that we know what's wrong with her, it's a matter of how well she takes to treatment."

"How bad...I mean...will she...?" I could not finish my question.

Dr. Costello frowned and looked me dead in the eye. "I'm not sure. It's possible, but I promise you, we will do everything we can to ensure that Shannon gets well again."

"Thank you," Jeannine said, her voice cracking.

It made me sick. How could someone who brings herself to a doctor for every sniffle, every ache, neglect to bring her own daughter to one when she's bitten by a wild bat? It wasn't for lack of insurance or knowledge. Jeannine had extensive knowledge of even the most obscure diseases and was always convinced she had one of them. She knew her way around the system. Why hadn't she brought Shannon to the doctor?

And what had she said to Shannon to make her not tell me? Why was Shannon willing to take this secret to the grave?

Shannon and I were close. During that summer, while she and her sisters had been visiting, she'd called me every day while I was at work.

"When are you coming home, Dad? Can you come home early today? Can you take tomorrow off?"

We'd talked every day when she wasn't staying with me. She had even told her sister, Barbara, that she wished she could live with me, but didn't want to upset her mother. She was such a good kid with a big heart. She didn't deserve to suffer like this because of her mother's selfish behavior. I still can't understand why Shannon didn't tell me about the bat bite.

"Jeannine," I said, trying to keep my voice and my temper under control, "where are Mary and Kristine?"

She clucked her tongue. "I told you—with a neighbor."

"Do you have a phone number and an address for me?"

"I don't know it off-hand. And I don't have my purse with me."

"Could you please get it to me by the end of the day?"

Jeannine rolled her eyes. "Sure."

There was nothing more Dr. Costello could tell us until he received the call from the doctors in Milwaukee, so we went inside the cubicle to tell Shannon.

She was awake, watching cartoons on the fuzzy TV screen, IVs dripping and an oxygen mask in place. I walked over to her side and took her hand.

"Hi, Shannon," Dr. Costello said. "We have some news for you. We did some tests and it looks like you have rabies. Remember the bat bite from last summer?"

Shannon glanced over at her mother, then back at the doctor. Slowly, she nodded. I gave her hand a squeeze to let her know it was all right.

Dr. Costello went on to explain a little more about the disease to all of us and told Shannon about the little girl in Wisconsin who had survived the same illness. He was confident that Shannon, as brave as she was, would survive as well. I tried to drink in as much information as I could, but all the while, I watched Shannon's eyes. She was terrified, but never let one tear fall. *Why isn't she crying?* I wondered to myself. *She knows how she got rabies—why won't she tell me?* I wanted to shout this out to anyone who would listen, but I kept it to myself.

Nurse Kate popped her head into the cubicle. "Dr. Costello, you have a call from Dr. Willaby in Milwaukee."

As the doctor left the room, I looked down into Shannon's face, stroking her hair.

"You're going to be all right. Just hang in there, okay, sweetheart? Everything's going to be okay."

It has to be, I thought. *It has to be.*

Rabies. Who, in this day and age, gets rabies? Why did this have to happen to my Shannon? It could have been prevented easily by one trip to the doctor, months ago—or even just one phone call to tell me what had happened. Instead, there we were, wondering if each breath would be the one that put Shannon too far into her disease for the doctors to be able to cure her. No parents should ever have to worry about their child that way, and no child should ever have to suffer like that from a one-hundred-percent treatable disease.

The last time a person contracted rabies in Indiana, I found out over the course of things, was in 1959—some forty-seven years before my Shannon was struck down by the disease. Because of this sensational aspect, the hospital staff warned us that the media would likely be all over the story. They also asked Jeannine and me not to talk to any reporters.

Apparently, the dummy did not get that message. Banned from the hospital for the duration of Shannon's stay, he had plenty of free time to hang around at home. One day, when a news crew from a local TV station showed up at their door, he was more than happy to fill them in on the whole situation. Mark was there at the time as well, and he immediately called Jeannine to let her know what was going on. She got the moron on the phone and flipped out on him, telling him not to tell the reporters anything. My guess? They didn't yet have their stories straight, and whatever they were hiding, she was afraid that her dumb-as-a-rock boyfriend would let it out.

Unfortunately for her, she was too late. Jimmie had already had his audience with the reporters and had told them all about the bat attacking Shannon. He admitted to seeing the animal himself and even to knocking it off of Shannon's arm.

When I heard about this confession, it just about put me over the edge. I was still unbelievably angry about the bat story, and about how flippantly the jerk talked about it—as though he were proud that he was the one who'd "rescued" Shannon from this mysterious creature. It seemed to me as though he were missing the big picture—the one in which the bat flew away and left its deadly mark on my ten-year-old daughter, and this man and my wife did nothing about it at all. That he claimed to be Shannon's stepfather was just more salt poured into my wounds. I couldn't believe what was happening to my family and me. I was living a nightmare.

CHAPTER THIRTEEN

Dr. Costello explained the protocol to Jeannine and me privately, first. It was not at all what I'd expected. I assumed Shannon would be given all sorts of medications at different intervals, which was somewhat true. However, the first step was to put her in a medically induced coma.

"Rabies attacks the brain," Dr. Costello said. "By putting her in a coma, we can slow the process. We should be able to get the medication by Saturday at the earliest, Monday at the latest."

"Monday?" I said. "Why so long?"

"It's an experimental drug, not approved by the Food and Drug Administration yet, and only available in Switzerland. In order to import it, we need the Center for Disease Control to confirm that she has rabies and approve it."

"I thought you said it was confirmed."

"It is…here. CDC approval will take a little longer. I'm sorry. There's nothing I can do."

I took a deep breath and pushed aside my temper. "I'm sorry. Thank you." I knew Dr. Costello and his team were doing everything within their power and then some. I just didn't like the waiting game. I felt as if every second was one we couldn't afford to waste. And Jeannine had wasted enough time already.

I was still so angry with her. I had spent the first four days in the hospital combing through my brain to find some seemingly insignificant event in the recess of my memory that may have provided some insight to Shannon's illness. And now I knew that Jeannine had conveniently "forgotten" a *bat bite*?

Dr. Costello, Jeannine and I went back in to explain things to Shannon. She was so pale and thin, with dark purple circles under her eyes. Jeannine went on one side of the bed, I went to the other, and we each took one of Shannon's hands. Wearily, she looked back and forth between us. I was sure that she could sense our tension.

Dr. Costello slowly and calmly explained to Shannon that she would be going to sleep for a little while so they could slow down the effect the rabies was having on her. He warned her that she might be asleep for quite a while, but when she woke up, she would feel better.

"And then your only problem will be catching up on all that homework you missed," he joked.

Shannon cracked a weak smile, and then her features relaxed to the same miserable expression she had held for the past few days. Smiling hurt her.

She was terrified and relieved at the same time. I could see it in her eyes. Sleep had not come easily for her in a few days, and whenever it did finally come, she never dozed for very long.

"It'll be all right, sweetheart," I whispered, giving her hand a squeeze.

She looked up at me. I felt as though she was searching my face for the truth.

Dr. Costello and his team did not waste any time. They began preparation for putting Shannon into the coma. My heart pounded harder in my chest with each passing second. Jeannine kissed Shannon's hand and then her cheek, her eyes glistening with tears.

"Sweet dreams, honey," Jeannine croaked. She then left the room, as if unable to bear seeing anymore.

I leaned over Shannon and wiped some hair away from her face. "Everything's going to be okay. And I'll be right here when you wake up."

Shannon nodded. I kissed her forehead. "I love you."

She couldn't answer, but she didn't have to.

I stayed in the room while the doctors hooked her up to various machines that would monitor her vitals and brain activity. It was all a blur to me—men and women in white coats gathered around the bed, checking this reading, starting that drip…and in the middle of it all was Shannon, covered in a white thermal blanket, her hair spread out across the pillow, an oxygen mask covering her face. She never took her eyes off of me. I wished I could read her mind. There were a million things going through mine.

Shannon closed her eyes and let out a slow breath. I waited. My heart was pounding. Seconds seemed like an eternity. As much as I trusted Dr. Costello and his team, the lingering fear was hard to push aside. She inhaled again, slowly.

The doctors monitored her for a little while and then left her in the care of the nurses. I stayed in the room for a little while longer, watching Shannon sleep and praying for a miracle—for the drug we needed to arrive as soon as possible.

I stood there for a long while. By the time I finally pulled myself from the room, Jeannine had left the hospital.

I went down to get myself yet another cup of coffee, and as soon as I reached an area with adequate reception, my cell phone rang. I was beginning to dread hearing the ring tone I had once thought was so catchy—it made me think of all the times Shannon had called that summer, asking me when I was getting home from work. I checked the caller ID. It was an anonymous number.

Probably another relative wondering what's going on, I thought.

I was so tired of explaining the story, bringing my blood to a boil over and over again at Jeannine's neglect, but the family had a right to know. With a sigh, I answered the call.

"Hello?" I said, surprised by how weary I sounded.

"Hi, Dad!" Barbara's cheerful voice resounded through the earpiece.

"Hi, sweetheart." A feeling of dread washed over me as a debate raged inside my head. Barbara was in the Bahamas on a vacation with some friends. She had worked at a part-time job all summer to save up for this trip. I didn't want her to worry and ruin her good time, but I didn't want to keep her in the dark, either.

"You okay?" she asked. "You sound upset or tired."

I hesitated. *She worked so hard,* I told myself. *Let her enjoy her vacation.* "Just tired. Didn't sleep much last night. How's the Bahamas?"

"It's beautiful down here! We went parasailing today—you know, it's not as much of a rush as I thought it would be. It's actually real quiet up there…"

Barbara didn't stay on the phone for very long. She only had a few minutes left on the calling card she had bought, and her friends were ready to go down to the hotel pool for a swim. She had just called to check in.

"We're going swimming now, Dad. I love you."

"I love you, too, sweetheart."

"Oh, and tell Shannon that I took lots of pictures when we went parasailing for her."

"I…I will." I nearly choked on my words. I hoped Barbara didn't notice anything.

"Bye, Dad!"

"Bye, honey," I said. Barbara hung up the phone.

I slumped down in a cafeteria chair and buried my face in my hands.

How could this have happened? What would possess Jeannine to keep the bat bite a secret? Why didn't she rush Shannon to the hospital that night? Why didn't Shannon tell me? We usually spoke at least three times a day. She was my heart.

She must have been told specifically not to tell me, or she probably would have brought it up. Whenever we'd talked, Shannon had always prattled on about everything that had happened in her day, from what Mary or Kristine had said at dinner to the play-by-play details of her baseball games.

I asked myself, over and over, *Why did this have to happen? Why my Shannon?* Every ounce of strength I had held on to over the last few days, for Shannon's sake, slipped from my grasp. My nose tingled; the lump rose in my throat. There, in the hospital cafeteria, I broke down and sobbed.

CHAPTER FOURTEEN

Any idiot knows to seek medical attention when they're bitten by a wild animal. Knowing Jeannine, she was probably drunk or filled with pills and didn't want to look bad to anyone working at the hospital. She jealously guarded her custody of the children. Even though we had agreed after she moved the first time that the three older children would live with me and the three youngest would live with her, she always seemed to be afraid that I would take them from her. If I brought the girls back late from my parenting weekend, she would be ready to call the police.

Now she had reason to fear. There was no way in hell I was going to let her keep Mary and Kristine when she—a hypochondriac who brought herself to the doctor for every minor sniffle—did not even consider bringing her own daughter to a doctor after a bat bite. What if Jeannine was the one who'd been attacked? I'd bet good money that she would have gone to the doctor to get a rabies shot that day, or at least within twenty-four hours.

I calmed myself down and blew my nose on a napkin. Then I called my lawyer. His secretary picked up the phone and told me he was in a meeting. I left a message with her and asked for him to call me back as soon as possible.

Taking a deep breath, I began to make my usual round of calls to family members, to let them know what was going on—both my family and Jeannine's. I told the same story over and over until I was numb. Nobody knew what to say. What *could* they say?

"I'm so sorry, Pat."

How do you respond to an apology? "Thank you"? "It's not your fault"? I tried to keep positive, and then rushed to the end of the phone conversation.

"I'll pray for her."

I appreciated this. We all needed to pray. But after hearing it a hundred times, the bitter, skeptical side of me began to wonder how much good praying would do if we didn't get the medication in time.

"Is there anything we can do?"

I asked plenty of friends and relatives living close by if I could call on them as last-minute babysitters for Mary and Kristine, and to check on Mark and Barbara from time to time. Everyone was more than happy to help.

"Do you need anything?"

Yes. Ribavirin A non-FDA-approved, experimental drug produced only in Switzerland. But we still had to wait on the CDC.

"Try to stay positive."

I promised I would do my best—and I would. I had to be strong. For my kids. For Shannon.

I didn't see Jeannine for the rest of the day. She never gave me the contact information for the neighbor Mary and Kristine were staying with—a court-ordered requirement when neither she nor I were available to take the kids. I called my deadbeat lawyer again and left yet another message with his secretary. What good was a court-ordered requirement, I wondered, if there were no consequences for it being broken?

I woke up Friday morning in my usual uncomfortable chair. Nurses had suggested that I stay at the Ronald McDonald House or even in the waiting room, where there were couches instead of hard, plastic chairs. But I was not quite ready to leave Shannon's side.

Nurse Kate entered.

"Morning," I whispered. I still wasn't used to the idea that my voice would not wake Shannon.

"Good morning," she said in a normal voice. "Did I wake you?"

"No," I said. "I was already awake."

I stretched and yawned, rubbing the nearly full beard on my face. I needed to shave. I needed to shower.

Dr. Costello appeared in the room to make his rounds. He spotted me and smiled.

"I just got off the phone with Dr. Willaby in Milwaukee. They have some leftover Ribavirin from when they treated Jeanna Giese. They're sending it over and we should have it by this afternoon."

I couldn't speak. A miracle. At last, some glimmer of hope!

Wide awake now, I looked over at Shannon. *It's going to be okay, honey. It's really going to be okay…*

"Have you been in touch with her mother?" I asked.

Dr. Costello shook his head. "I haven't seen her yet this morning."

She was probably still asleep, but I kept that assumption to myself. While Dr. Costello and his team went about making their rounds, I went down to the cafeteria to make a dozen or so phone calls.

I called my lawyer again first. He was still not available. I left another message and then called my son, Mark.

"Does Barbara know about anything?" he asked after I gave him the update.

"No. She called yesterday, but I didn't tell her anything yet. I'll fill her in when she gets home tomorrow."

"Are you going to be here when she gets home?"

"I'm not sure. Depends on how Shannon's doing."

He paused. "Dad?"

"Yes?"

"Is…" His voice cracked. "Is Shannon going to make it?"

The lump returned to my throat. "I pray to God she does," I said. "I really pray to God."

I made phone calls to Peter, my family, most of Jeannine's family, some friends and some neighbors. With the adults, I discussed getting the other kids vaccinated against rabies, "just in case," and spreading that word to Shannon's friends' and classmates' parents as well. With my children, I updated them on Shannon's condition and then listened to them talk about their own days, their own activities. Something in the normalness of it was soothing.

And then, I tried my lawyer again. I still did not reach him. By the time I finished updating everybody, it was well past noon. I ordered myself a cup of lukewarm chicken noodle soup and some coffee. Just as I sat down to force myself to eat lunch, I saw Jeannine coming out of the gift shop, a vase of flowers in her arms. She had just arrived at the hospital.

Furious as I was with her, I had to tell her about the Ribavirin. "Jeannine!" I called. She ignored me. Leaving my soup and coffee where it was, I hurried after her. I finally caught up with her at the elevator. I told her everything Dr. Costello had told me that morning.

"Oh, thank God," she said, clutching her heart with her free hand. Her purse strap slipped from her shoulder down to her elbow, and it caught my eye.

"You have your purse with you," I said, nodding toward it. "Could I please have the phone number and address where Mary and Kristine are?"

Jeannine clucked her tongue and shoved the vase of flowers into my arms. "Here," she snapped. "Hold this."

She dug around in her purse for a minute and pulled out a little scrap of paper and a pen. She wrote down a phone number, handed me the scrap of paper, and then yanked the flowers back.

"And the address?" I asked as the elevator doors opened.

"Pat, I don't *know* it offhand. Jesus! Can't you concentrate on Shannon?" Jeannine stormed down the hall ahead of me, her heels clicking on the floor.

Fuming, I let her go on ahead. Couldn't *I* concentrate on Shannon? This from the woman who did not bring her own daughter to the doctor after a bat bite? How *dare* she!

But I had no desire to get kicked out of the hospital when Shannon lay in a coma, fighting for her life. I pushed my anger aside and walked back to the PICU as slowly as I possibly could.

Jeannine fawned over Shannon, holding her hand, sobbing, talking to her, but she did not stay for long. She was gone by three p.m.

After Jeannine left, I called my lawyer again…and left another message.

The Ribavirin arrived from Milwaukee and was administered to Shannon almost immediately. Dr. Costello and his team milled about, checking her vital signs, monitoring her, taking more blood samples and bringing me cups of coffee.

Jeannine returned at around six o'clock, arms laden with another bouquet and a huge teddy bear.

"Where were you?" I asked.

She sniffed and stuck her nose in the air. "*I* was in the gift shop. I don't see *you* spending any money on flowers and teddy bears for her."

I bit my tongue to hold back a retort. I was not about to play these childish games with her. "Jeannine, how could you forget a bat bite?"

She glared at me. "I already told you. I just did. You forget things all the time, Pat, in case you've forgotten *that*!"

Taking out the trash, the occasional birthday—once I forgot our anniversary. Never anything like this. Not when it came to my kids' health and safety. I didn't believe her, but arguing about it wasn't going to do any of us any good.

"Do you have that address for me?"

"No."

"Could you go get it?"

"I'll get it later."

After that, Jeannine and I ignored each other until she left—just before seven-thirty p.m. She was always gone by seven-thirty p.m.

After Jeannine left, Dr. Costello pulled me aside. He and the staff at the hospital had determined that for the comfort of the other patients and their families, as well as the staff and Jeannine and me, it would probably be best if Jeannine and I visited Shannon in rotation. I'd sit with her for two hours, then Jeannine, then me and so on. I didn't like the sound of it, but I had to admit that it was getting harder to control my temper around Jeannine. This was her doing. She took herself to the doctor for the slightest ailment, real or imaginary, but couldn't be bothered to do the same for her own daughter after she was attacked by a bat in the middle of the night. I couldn't be near her without shooting daggers her way or snapping comments. I wasn't proud of my behavior, but I knew the rotation was probably the best solution.

Dr. Costello thanked me for my understanding and told me he had already discussed this with Jeannine. Then he said, "Shannon's stable, at least. There's not much that can be done as of right now. You've been here for a week and I know you have other children, so this might be a good opportunity to take advantage of this lull and spend time with them."

Since it was my parenting weekend and since Mary and Kristine were with a neighbor of Jeannine's who I didn't know, I did not need to be told twice. Besides, Barbara was due home the next day, and I wanted to tell her everything in person.

I said a quick goodbye to Shannon and gave Dr. Costello my cell phone number in case anything changed—good or bad. On my way out of the hospital, I called Mark to let him know that I would be home when Barbara arrived, and that Mary and Kristine would be there as well.

"If I can find them," I said, unable to keep my bitter tone under control. "I had to practically extract a phone number from your mother, and she didn't give me an address at all."

"What neighbor are they with?"

"Someone named Tammy." I paused as I reached my car and pulled the piece of paper out of my pocket. I read the phone number off to Mark.

"Oh, yeah. Tammy Brown. I've met her before. She and her husband are nice people."

"Still, I don't know them and it would be nice to know where my children are in case of an emergency. Do you know where they live?"

Mark gave me the address and some basic directions. I thanked him and got off the phone so I could call Tammy Brown and let her know I was coming. Though I was still worried sick about Shannon, I was looking forward to seeing my other children, taking a hot shower, shaving, and sleeping in a real bed.

Pray, I reminded myself. *Keep praying. It'll be all right. You got the medication early. She's going to be all right.*

I really believed myself, and that God would not let her die. That He would not take her away from her brothers and sisters and me. "Please, God," I prayed.

I called up the Browns on my way to their house, to introduce myself and let them know that I was coming to pick up the girls.

Tammy sounded apprehensive. "Well…um…it's all right, you know. The girls are more than welcome to stay here."

"Thank you, but I'm already on my way."

"It's not any trouble at all."

"Thank you, but I'd really like to see my children. It's my parenting weekend, anyway."

When I hung up the phone, I was annoyed. Why was this woman so reluctant to let me have my children back?

When I picked up Mary and Kristine, they were fed, bathed, dressed and ready to go, which was more than I could say for the times I'd picked them up from Jeannine herself. It was always something with her: they couldn't find their shoes, they were in the middle of picking up their toys, they hadn't finished breakfast—or, rather, Jeannine had not made them any yet. The Browns, however, still seemed unsure if they should allow me to take my daughters. They told me I could visit them there so that the girls did not have to travel around so much.

"It's all right. My oldest daughter is coming home from a vacation tomorrow. I'm sure they'll want to see her."

They offered to take the girls again after my parenting weekend was over.

I politely declined their offer. "No, thank you. I've already made arrangements with my brother and his wife."

That wasn't quite true. Though my brother's wife had offered to watch Mary and Kristine at a moment's notice, I had not quite made official arrangements with them just yet. The Browns seemed nice, but the fact remained that I did not know them, and I'd feel more comfortable if people I knew were caring for my children—especially over an extended period of time.

Finally conceding, the Browns said goodbye to Mary and Kristine, telling them to call if they needed anything. What had Jeannine told them about me so that they did not want these girls to go with their own father?

I made sure Mary and Kristine were buckled in and then I drove off, asking them questions about their week and what they had done while at the Browns' house.

Kristine had drawn several pictures for my refrigerator, and Mary had worked on her cartwheels—a skill that Shannon had been trying to teach her. Kristine had worked on tying her shoes, and Mary had read a few Dr. Seuss books all by herself. They prattled on about what they'd done, where they'd slept, the Browns' dog—everything. It was soothing to hear their voices.

"Where's Shannon?" Kristine asked after telling me all about what was on *Sesame Street* that morning.

The knot tightened in my stomach again. "I…Shannon is still very sick, sweetheart. She's in the hospital."

"Oh." She considered this for a moment. "Can we go see her?"

"Not right now. Maybe sometime next week. She's…sleeping right now."

How do you explain a medically induced coma to a four-year-old? The only thing they knew about rabies was from *Old Yeller*, and I was not about to conjure up that image. Plus, I knew that I could not explain the situation to anyone without bad-mouthing Jeannine and getting angry again. And I just wanted to spend some nice, calm time with Mary and Kristine.

"You know," I said, "Barbara's coming home tomorrow. You guys will see her when she gets dropped off. She said she took a lot of pictures."

Mary and Kristine then began firing off questions about Barbara and her trip. Where had she gone? What was it like there? Could we go on vacation there next year? Did I think Barbara had brought them back anything?

Mary and Kristine talked themselves to sleep as I drove down the highway, back to Oak Lawn. Without their pleasant chatter to distract me, the familiar hollow feeling returned to my stomach.

Mark met me down at my car when I reached my apartment.

"Pete called," he said. "Said his friend's going to bring him to the hospital tomorrow. He tried to call your cell, but it went right to voice mail."

"Thanks. My cell battery died on the way home."

I probably wouldn't have picked up, anyway. I didn't like to drive and talk on the phone, especially with my kids in the car.

Mark helped me carry the girls up to bed. As I pulled the blankets over them, I looked down at their faces. They were safe for now, with me. If only Shannon had been with me when she'd been bitten. If only she had said something to me. What if something happened to Mary or Kristine? Jeannine was known to repeat her mistakes. Neighbors had told me that Mary, Kristine and even Shannon and Barbara had wandered out of the house and around the neighborhood when they were just beginning to toddle around. Jeannine did not keep a close enough watch on them. I could not trust her to keep them out of harm's way.

I made a mental note to call my lawyer the following morning. I kissed Mary and Kristine goodnight, then took a long, hot shower. Standing there, the steam rising and the water beating down on me, I began to sob. My Shannon, my sweet, beautiful Shannon, was in a coma. Who knew if she would ever wake up? Would I ever be able to look into my little girl's eyes again?

Any parent knows that when your child is born, you feel a love that you never thought was possible. Every single one of my children had made my heart swell to the point where I felt as if I could burst all over. No parent should ever have to face the fear of losing a child. It is far too cruel a punishment.

How could Jeannine let this happen?

I stayed in the shower until the hot water ran out.

CHAPTER FIFTEEN

Even though I was finally home, lying down, free from the chill of the hospital, it took me forever to get to sleep. I worried about something happening to Shannon while I was away from her. I worried about what would happen to Mary and Kristine if I could not get custody. And I wondered how in the world I was going to explain everything to Barbara.

It was close to Halloween by then, and I couldn't stand the site of those fake bats everywhere. This was probably why, when sleep did come to me, I dreamed of Shannon, sleeping on a hospital bed, bats swirling all around her while Mary and Kristine ran about, trying to catch them. I tried to run up to them to stop them, but Jeannine and the jerk blocked my way, refusing to let me by.

I woke up not feeling refreshed at all, but smiled as soon as I opened my eyes. Mary was hovering over me, giggling.

"Hi, Daddy. Can we have pancakes for breakfast?" For a second, I thought it was like any other weekend...then, I remembered everything.

The morning went by too fast. I called my lawyer right after breakfast, and as I expected, there was no answer, so I left a message. His office was, I assumed, closed for the weekend.

That afternoon, Mary and Kristine stood side by side looking out the window of my apartment, waiting for Barbara's friend's mother to pull up and drop her off. They giggled to each other, wondering if each car was *the* car.

I watched them from the kitchen doorway, the image from my dream still swirling around in my mind. They were still under Jeannine's care. What if, in her neglect, something happened to one of them? My Shannon was already struggling for her life.

"She's here! She's here!" Mary called out.

"She's here!" Kristine repeated.

I joined them at the window and looked down to see a white minivan sitting idle in the street. Tanned and beaming, Barbara stepped out of the side door, duffel bag in hand. She leaned back inside the van and hugged her friend and then, waving as the van drove away, she hurried inside.

I opened the door before she reached it. Mary and Kristine rushed her. She dropped her duffel bag and scooped Kristine up onto her hip. After giving her a kiss on the cheek, Barbara set her down and did the same for Mary. Then she turned to me.

"Hi, Dad!" she said, hugging me tightly.

"Hi, sweetheart. How was your trip?"

"Great! When we got there the first day, it was drizzling a little bit, but it cleared up by the time we were settled in the hotel…"

Barbara started to tell me all about snorkeling, about how clear the ocean was and how nice the resort was. Then, halfway through telling me about her second day there, she stopped.

"Where's Shannon?"

My face must have fallen, because so did Barbara's.

"What?" she asked. "What's the matter?"

"Sweetheart, don't get upset—I didn't tell you because I didn't want you to worry while you were on vacation."

"What?" Barbara asked again, her voice becoming more frantic.

"Shannon's in the hospital."

"She's *what*? Is she okay? What's wrong with her?"

"She has rabies. She was bitten by a bat early this summer—your mother 'forgot' about it." I could not keep the bite out of my voice. "Right now, she's in a medically induced coma—stable, for the time being. But for now, there's nothing we can do."

Barbara's eyes filled with tears and she stared at a spot on the floor. I felt awful for dropping that information on her. She was excited. She just came back from a trip. She should have been laughing, telling Mary, Kristine, Shannon and me all about it, calling up other friends, showing off souvenirs. "That's why your phone was turned off so much this week," she whispered, a few tears dripping down her cheeks.

"Yes."

"Is she going to be all right?"

I hesitated. "I'm not sure. I hope so."

"Where's Mark? And Peter?"

"Mark's at a friend's house." He had left around noon. "Pete's at the hospital now. A friend drove him."

"And Mom?"

"I'm not sure, sweetheart."

Barbara looked away.

"I'm sorry I didn't tell you sooner."

"No...I know why you didn't. I wish you did, but I'm glad you didn't, but I...I don't know." Her face scrunched up and she buried her face in my shoulder, sobbing. I just hugged her. There was nothing more I could do.

After Barbara calmed down a little and I promised to take her to see Shannon as soon as possible, we were all able to enjoy the day together. Barbara had brought each of her siblings a souvenir from the Bahamas, had taken tons of pictures, and she told us all about the great time she had. Mark came home late that afternoon and joined us for dinner. When I put Mary and Kristine to bed, I told them that they would be going to Aunt Sara and Uncle Charles' house the next day.

"Why can't we stay with you, Daddy?" Mary asked.

"Because I have to go to the hospital and see about Shannon."

"Can we come?"

"No. Not tomorrow. Maybe sometime next week."

Next week. Next month. How long would she be in the hospital?

I kissed Mary and Kristine good night, tucked them in, then called my brother and asked if I could drop the girls off the next day. He and his wife agreed.

"I'm not sure how long I'll need you to take them for, though," I said.

"Pat, just take care of what you need to take care of. Don't worry about Mary and Kristine. We'll take them for as long as you need us to."

"Thanks."

Mark, Barbara and I stayed up late watching TV and talking about Shannon's condition. I tried not to bash Jeannine, but there was no denying my anger and bitterness. My tone said it all.

Early Sunday afternoon, as we were finishing up lunch, I received a call from Riley Hospital, asking my permission to allow Jeannine's sisters, Cassie and Carrie, to see Shannon. Ever since the drama with Jimmie, no one was allowed to see her unless they had permission from both Jeannine and me. I granted it and hoped they would still be there when I returned to the hospital that evening. I could use some company.

After lunch, I dropped Mary and Kristine off, thanked my brother and sister-in-law about a hundred times, gave them the names and numbers of other family members, just in case, and went back to Riley. When I arrived that evening, I found someone else familiar waiting outside the PICU.

"Jolene?"

Jeannine's niece, Jolene, had flown in from New York. With everything else going on, I didn't remember her telling me she was coming.

"Hi, Pat. How are you?"

After hugs, greetings and a quick update, I asked, "How long have you been here?"

"I arrived around the same time last night, stayed in a hotel and got here this morning," she said.

"I'm sorry. I completely forgot you were coming. I was home with Mary and Kristine and—"

"You don't have to explain. You were with your kids. They need you, too." "Have you seen Cassie and Carrie?"

She nodded. "Yeah. They're in with Shannon right now."

Jeannine and Jolene, who had always been close, had a falling out following Jolene's attempt to talk Jeannine out of divorcing me. That seemed to be Jeannine's pattern—any time someone would confront her out of concern and love, she'd push them away. She refused to believe that, perhaps, she was the root of her own problems. To her, it was always everyone else who was to blame.

"I did see Jeannine, though," Jolene said. "This morning."

"Oh?"

"It was closer to afternoon, but yes. Cassie, Carrie and I were told she was staying in the Ronald McDonald House, so we figured we'd wait for her to arrive to go in. I know she usually sleeps until noon, but I figured with her daughter being sick, since she knew we were coming, she would at least be awake. At noon, she still wasn't here, so the three of us went down to get her."

"Was she awake?" I asked.

"Oh, she was awake," Jolene fumed. "But she wasn't even dressed. She was sitting around in her *bathrobe*!" Jolene's hands flailed about as she talked. "Telling some other person with a sick child all about when Shannon was bitten, she didn't tell anyone and just went to sleep on the couch and how if *only* Shannon had said something when it had happened." Jolene clucked her tongue in disgust. "Soliciting sympathy from some random stranger when she should have been up here with her child."

I said nothing. That was the third version of the bat story I had heard. Jeannine had told doctors and nurses that she'd run into the room when she'd heard Shannon screaming, thrown a blanket over her and carried her out of the room. She had told one of the orderlies that she'd seen the cat carrying something in its mouth that she thought was a bird. I didn't care what the real story was. All I cared about was Shannon getting well again.

"We tried to sit her down and have a rational talk with her," Jolene continued, "but of course, it didn't go too well. She said that she has to stay at the Ronald McDonald House because of her back pain."

I sighed. "Well, she always did complain of back pain. That's why she's taking methadone and OxyContin."

"Where are Mary and Kristine now?" Jolene asked. "Jeannine said they were with you."

"They were. Now they're with my brother and his wife. Do you remember them?"

"I think I met them before."

"Well, they said they'd keep them for as long as I needed. I told them to call Cassie if they needed help."

Jeannine's sister, Cassie, lived in Chicago, not too far from my brother. She, too, had offered to watch the girls at a moment's notice.

"After seeing Jeannine like that, I came back here. I was absolutely disgusted. She finally showed up an hour later, red-eyed and carrying a teddy bear for Shannon's room."

"Is she in there now?"

Jolene snorted. "Jeannine? No. She left about an hour ago."

Cassie and Carrie emerged from the PICU moments later. We hugged. I filled them in on everything, including where Mary and Kristine were. We prayed together. We talked about happier things to get our minds off of the situation a little. We talked for about an hour and then, all too soon, Cassie and Carrie had to go.

Jolene stayed for the weekend. She made sure that I ate full meals and even occasionally went to the Ronald McDonald House to push Jeannine out the door and try to convince her to give permission for her to go in and see her little cousin. Jolene often came back fuming.

My lawyer did not call me the next day. He did not call me by the end of the week. I continued to call him three times a day, every day. On Friday, when I once again did not get in touch with him, I left him one final message: I would be seeking other representation.

Within a day or two of securing a new lawyer, I had a date for an emergency custody hearing: October 15, 2006. When the day came, though, I just couldn't tear myself away from Shannon to make it. To drive from Riley's to Valparaiso, Indiana, where the court was would have taken about six hours round-trip; add in the actual court time, and I just could not fathom being gone for that long. Shannon wasn't getting any better, her vitals were deteriorating and I couldn't leave her. So, my lawyer moved for it to be pushed back, and I just had to wait to be assigned a new court date. I was certain that any reasonable person would award me full custody of Kristine, Mary and Shannon after hearing about Jeannine's neglect.

CHAPTER SIXTEEN

Monday, October 16, 2006, ten o'clock p.m. Charles and Sara Carroll sat on their couch, watching some late night TV and unwinding. At a commercial, Sara tapped Charles' leg and announced that she was going to head to bed. Just as she stood up, there was a knock at the door.

Sara and Charles exchanged a look of confusion. Who could be at their door at ten p.m.? The person knocked again. Charles answered it.

Two uniformed police officers stood in the doorway. Charles glanced behind him and saw a patrol car sitting in his driveway.

"Hi, folks," one of the cops said.

"Hello," Charles said.

"Sorry to bother you so late, but there's a woman sitting in a car down the street who says you have her kids."

Sara appeared at Charles' shoulder and invited the officers inside.

"We're watching our nieces while my brother is at the hospital with his other daughter."

"This woman claims that her children were not brought back after her ex-husband's parenting weekend."

Sara sighed. "They were just not brought back to her neighbor's house. Jeannine, we assumed, would be at the hospital all week—especially since she doesn't work." She explained the situation to the police officers: Shannon's illness, her coma and my decision to bring Mary and Kristine to people who both Jeannine and I knew well. For additional assurance, Sara called Jeannine's sister, Cassie, who came right over.

Cassie talked to the officers and backed up Sara's and Charles' statements. Satisfied, the cops thanked Charles and Sara and apologized again for disturbing them so late.

"When we pulled up to her car," one of the officers said, referring to Jeannine's, "it was billowing smoke. It was rusty, dirty and broken down. I wasn't sure how much of a waste of time this was going to be, but she made the call and we had to look into it."

"Oh, I understand," Sara said as she walked the police officers to the door. "What I want to know is why she's worrying about children who are perfectly safe when she has a daughter in a coma in the hospital."

One of the cops shrugged. "I was wondering that myself."

"If she comes on my property, I want her arrested."

"I'll let her know. Good night, ma'am."

I learned about the incident the following afternoon—first from Cassie and then from Sara when I called them from the hospital to give them the daily update. I could only sigh and shake my head. I stared at the turkey sandwich I had bought from the cafeteria; I'd only eaten half of it. The bread was soggy and the turkey almost tasteless, but I was hungry; rather, I still had no appetite, but I had to force myself to eat.

"At least the police left Mary and Kristine with you, where I know they're safe," I told Sara. "Are you sure you'll be able to watch them for a while?"

"Well, I spoke to Cassie and she agreed to watch them if for any reason Charles and I can't," Sara said.

"Thanks. I appreciate that."

Jeannine's family was very trustworthy and family oriented. I knew my children were in good hands. They would be safer with anyone but Jeannine.

As soon as I hung up with Sara, my phone rang again. It was Karen Gould, an old next-door neighbor from when we'd lived in Chicago. She had heard that the girls were staying with my brother and wanted to make sure I passed her contact information along in case they needed help watching the girls.

"Word travels fast," I told her.

"Well, I talked to John Ferris this morning—remember him?"

John was the son of another old neighbor from Chicago. He'd lived on the other side of us and was a good kid—very friendly, always ready to lend a hand. "Yeah, I remember him," I said.

"Well, he said that Jeannine called, looking for his dad to give her a ride back to her motel late last night, but he was already sleeping. So John went to pick her up."

"Oh?"

"Pat, there's something wrong with Jeannine. Have you seen her yet today?" Karen said.

"Jeannine hasn't been in the hospital since Sunday night."

"Well, John told me that they got to talking as he drove and she confided in him that she's on methadone."

I sighed. "I know."

"She also apparently invited him up to her room when he dropped her off. He said she reeked of booze and was probably on something else, too."

"Oh, Jesus."

"Pat, she was driving like that, looking to pick up her children. You have to do something."

"I know. I'm trying!" I snapped.

I had called my lawyer three times the day before and once that morning. When I got off the phone with Karen, I called him again.

Still no answer.

Still no call back.

This was really getting on my nerves.

The day before Jolene was scheduled to fly back home, I came out of the PICU early in the afternoon and found her pacing in the waiting room. Her cell phone was up to her ear and she was writing something down on the back of a receipt.

"Anything else you can think of?" She looked up as I entered the room and nodded to me. "Mmm hmm…okay. Thanks. Call me later if you can think of anything… Okay… Bye."

"Work?" I asked as she hung up the phone.

"No. Mark."

"Mark? My Mark?"

"Yeah. I got back from seeing Jeannine a little while ago and got a confession from her. Did you know she's on antidepressants?"

"Doesn't surprise me," I said.

"And muscle relaxants. And pain medication—oh, but not just any pain medication. *Methadone.*"

"She actually told you all of this on her own?"

"Of course not. I walked into her room and caught her on the phone with one of her doctors. She was trying to get a refill on her prescription, but apparently, the doctor refused. She was arguing that she takes so many pills a day and it does nothing for her—and she's getting pretty nasty, too." Jolene glanced over the receipt she had been writing on and stuck it in her wallet.

"What's that?" I asked.

"A list of all the medications Peter and Mark have seen her take. Isn't methadone what they give heroin addicts to give them their fix?" she asked.

I nodded.

"I confronted her about what I heard her saying on the phone, Pat, and of course she had an excuse for everything. And now, she's furious with me. She called the nurses and told them that I would never be allowed to visit with Shannon."

I shook my head. I didn't know what else to say.

"She has a serious problem," Jolene went on. "She should *not* have custody of Mary and Kristine."

"I know. I'm working on it." I told her about my attempts to call my lawyer.

Jolene frowned. "You might need to switch lawyers if he doesn't call you back, Pat. Ask around. See if anyone can suggest a name or two."

While Jolene was there, she did everything she could to get Jeannine to grant her permission to see Shannon. It was never given. She spent a lot of time with me in the waiting room, keeping me company and sometimes making various phone calls on my behalf if I felt too weary to call everyone and give them updates.

Jeannine continued to show up at the hospital periodically, though more often, she didn't. She would go days without seeing her daughter and while I was grateful for her absence, I felt disgusted that she would take off like that when Shannon was in a coma. What could possibly have been more important than this? Mary and Kristine were still at my brother's house, so she was not taking care of them. Mark, Barbara and Pete had not even heard from her.

CHAPTER SEVENTEEN

Every doctor on Dr. Costello's team was fantastic—especially Dr. Costello himself. I cannot even begin to describe how thankful I was that Shannon was his patient. I always felt confident that he and his team were doing everything they possibly could for her.

On Wednesday at around nine-thirty p.m., as I was headed back to the PICU after grabbing something to eat, I heard laughter coming from down the hall, near the elevators. I knew before I even looked: Jeannine was back. And she was carrying another vase of flowers.

Her friend, Pam, was with her. Pam lived in Wisconsin and was one of Jeannine's "party girl" friends from way back. Both were giggling and shushing each other. Neither was walking straight. I shook my head and went back to the PICU.

Jeannine and Pam arrived a minute later, still suppressing laughter. When they entered Shannon's room, Pam held back at the door a little bit and whispered something to Jeannine.

"No, it's fine," Jeannine said. "You're not going to wake her up."

I clenched my teeth and kept my mouth shut. Jeannine walked around to Shannon's meal table and found a spot for the flowers she had brought. As she walked past me, I clenched my fists. She reeked of booze.

Pam was a thin woman, though not nearly as thin as Jeannine, with long curly hair and a tattoo on the small of her back that she always made sure was exposed. She kept staring at Shannon, wide-eyed, as if she were seeing something else that wasn't there. *She's probably on something*, I thought. And if Pam was on it, chances were Jeannine was on it, too. She never did like to be left out of anything.

I stood up and left the room to make some phone calls and begin the rotation. Pam and I made eye contact and nodded to each other, but that was the extent of it. I didn't say a word to Jeannine.

I spent two hours down in the lobby, sitting on the chairs near the gift shop, watching people move in and out of the revolving doors. One couple in particular caught my eye. There was a little boy with them, around Shannon's age. He was so pale, his skin was almost see-through; he wore a Cubs baseball cap and had the look of a cancer patient. But he was smiling. His parents were beaming. The heaviness of worry was absent from their faces and postures. The chemotherapy must have been working. They were going home. I hoped to God that I, too, could walk out that door with Shannon by my side, ready to take her to Taco Bell to celebrate.

Pete called me, interrupting my daydream. I wiped my eyes. I had not even realized I'd been crying.

He was off from work that weekend; his friend had agreed to drive him to the hospital to visit Shannon, and they needed directions. I talked with him for a little while and then called Mark and Barbara to check up on them. I had asked a neighbor to peek in on them from time to time, to make sure everything was all right, but I preferred to hear it directly from my kids.

After my nightly check-in, I checked my watch. I still had half an hour before my two-hour rotation. I dug around in my pockets for change to buy a cup of coffee.

I had been laid off back in August, and since my bills were minimal, I had been taking my time looking for a new job. In the meantime, I'd been delivering pizzas. The relative unemployment was both a blessing and a curse—it gave me as much time off as I needed to be with Shannon, but money was tight in the meantime.

At eleven-thirty p.m., I went back up to the PICU. As I reached Shannon's room, Pam and Jeannine nearly stumbled out the door. Nurse Kate walked by and raised an eyebrow at me. I just shook my head in disgust, then went back in to sit with Shannon.

Hospitals—no matter how friendly the staff, no matter how busy and bustling the hallways—are the loneliest of places. Friends and family can support you in a time of need, but they can't be there with you *all* the time. They have lives, jobs, school and other obligations. It's not a lack of compassion or concern; they simply cannot be there twenty-four hours a day.

But when your child is sick, in a coma, hanging on to her life by a thread, you toss everything out the window to be there by her side as much as you possibly can. For all of her faults, and as much as she infuriated me, I expected Jeannine to be there. She had no job, no obligations since Mary and Kristine were still at my brother's house—but apparently, her life with Jimmie was more important. She would pop in from time to time for an hour or two, disappear, then resurface at around five p.m. or so.

Jolene flew out from New York twice more, on weekends. Jeannine still refused to grant her visitation with Shannon, so I spoke to someone at the hospital and explained the situation— basically, I told this woman that Jeannine was nuts, and that there was no reason for what she was doing to Jolene other than spite. By the following weekend, Jolene was finally allowed to see Shannon, though only while Jeannine wasn't around.

Peter—then living on his own—was at the hospital whenever he could be; the friend who drove him even picked up Mark and Barbara and brought them along sometimes. But for the most part, I was alone with Shannon and my cell phone. It was my link, my lifeline, my only reminder that there was a world outside of spinal taps, IV drips, white thermal blankets and bone-chilling cold.

But after a while, I had nothing to say. There were good days, bad days and days with absolutely no change. I spent most of my time sitting beside Shannon, watching the little green lines on the various monitors, memorizing the numbers for her vitals so I knew what was normal and what was not. My heart skipped beats at any change in the pattern—particularly the one on the monitor that displayed her brainwave activity—but it usually fell right back into the same steady *blip…blip…blip…*

I rubbed my eyes and yawned. I had to take a break from watching the monitors or I would drive myself insane. I checked the clock on my cell phone. Eleven-fifteen a.m. Jeannine was still nowhere to be found.

My stomach gurgled. I hadn't eaten anything since Nurse Kate had brought me a sandwich the night before, just after Jeannine had left, so I went down to the cafeteria to force myself to eat something again and to make some phone calls to the outside world.

I still didn't have much of an appetite, so I ordered my default chicken noodle soup and went to sit down at my usual table, tucked in the far corner of the cafeteria.

I flipped open my phone and began to scroll through my address book. In general, if I had nothing really to report, I didn't call the people I knew were working. I didn't want to alarm them.

I scrolled down and paused on the name *Elaine*. With the hundreds of phone calls I had been making, I hadn't spoken to her since before we'd discovered Shannon had rabies. Feeling a little guilty, I hit the call button and put the phone to my ear.

One ring.

Two rings.

"Hello?"

"Hi, Elaine."

"Pat! How's Shannon? What's going on? Is everything okay?"

"Everything's stable for the moment. Sorry I haven't called you in a while. I've just—"

"Don't apologize. I'm sure you've had a million people to call," Elaine said. "I heard about Shannon having rabies. I'm so sorry, Pat. Do you know what bit her?"

"A bat."

Elaine gasped. "How did that happen?"

"I'm not sure. I've heard several different versions of the story."

I told her about Jeannine's memory lapse and the variations I had heard so far on what had happened.

"Unbelievable," Elaine said. "Though I shouldn't be surprised a bat got in. After you left, Shannon used to come over to my house a lot to spend the night because there was a mouse in her room. Jeannine always claimed to have gotten rid of it, but Shannon would find mouse poop in there some days and not want to sleep there at night."

My heart sank. Yet another thing I did not know about.

"I just…" I started, searching for the right words. "I don't understand it. Why didn't Shannon tell me? We talked so often…" My voice cracked and I broke down again.

When I finally calmed down, Elaine reassured me that there was nothing wrong with the relationship I had with Shannon. "She adores you, Pat. She probably didn't say anything because of Jeannine."

I knew it was true. My relationship with my daughter was solid. I just could not help but think, *If only she had told me.* I would have brought her to the doctor right away and been sure that she received the medical attention she needed. She wouldn't be here now. She would be laughing and playing, not in a coma. Why hadn't she told me?

I knew that Jeannine didn't like that Shannon called me so often. A neighbor once told me that Shannon confided in them that Jeannine told her she'd be sorry if she kept calling me all the time—making me seem like a bad person so my own children would grow up viewing me as the enemy.

Ever since Jeannine had begun this absurd quest for her "happiness," my children had suffered. She had confused them by assigning them various fake "aunts" and "uncles," calling the children of their neighborhood their "cousins." She had neglected them to the point of allowing them to have poor hygiene, visible cavities, ill-fitting clothing and no restrictions or discipline. She was not raising our children. She was allowing them to exist.

"Do the doctors see progress?" Elaine asked.

"Some days," I said. "Other days, it really doesn't look good. Three days ago, she had her last rites read to her." Elaine let out a gasp. "I thought I'd lost her—but she survived the night, and Dr. Costello said there was vast improvement the next day. Yesterday, she had a little dip, but today she's stable. It's up and down."

"My God…"

There was a moment where neither of us said anything. I crunched up a package of crackers and emptied the crumbs into my soup.

"What about you?" Elaine said, breaking the silence. "How are you holding up through all this?"

I sighed. "This is the hardest thing I've ever had to go through."

"I can't even imagine. How are the doctors? And the hospital staff?"

"They're great. I can't even begin to tell you how happy I am with the care they've given Shannon and me. You can really tell they're doing everything they possibly can. Her main doctor, Dr. Costello, is going out of his way to make sure everything is set for when he goes to Puerto Rico in two weeks."

"Puerto Rico?"

"I just found out this morning. His mother is sick. He's had this trip planned for a while to go visit her, but the rest of his team is going to be here and he's given them—and me—his cell phone number, just in case. My jaw dropped when he told me, but what can I do? It's his mother. And I'm sure in his line of work, there are always sick children that are in desperate need of his attention."

"True. I'm surprised Jeannine hasn't thrown a fit about that. She was never one to really care about other people's problems."

"I don't think Jeannine knows about it. She's only met Dr. Costello a few times. I've barely seen her."

Elaine clucked her tongue. "You've got to be kidding me! Her daughter is in the hospital, she doesn't work, and she's barely been there? Has she been with Mary and Kristine?"

"They're at my brother's house."

"Unbelievable. Well, the little ones are much better off there than with Jeannine. You know I've called Child Protective Services on her a few times, right?"

"I remember hearing her accusing me once of conspiring with you about that. But the phone call was breaking up, so I had no idea what she was talking about." I took a spoonful of my soup. It was piping hot and though it scalded my tongue, it was already beginning to warm my entire body.

"She's been careless and irresponsible for about as long as I've known her, but it got worse after she made you move out. She never woke up with the kids."

That I knew. Once, when I'd called the house, Kristine had picked up the phone. Jeannine had still been in bed and when I'd asked Kristine who was watching her, she'd said, "No one." Shannon had been at school already and had once again spent the night over at Elaine's—which she was doing at least three times a week, whenever Jeannine and Jimmie were drinking, getting high, fighting or all of the above.

"There were so many times," Elaine continued, "when I saw Mary or Kristine wandering around outside, no supervision, playing in the street. Whenever I brought them home, Jeannine always just said, 'Oh, thank you.' But it always happened again. You know, Michelle once pulled Mary out of the street just before a car hit her? I freaked out—Michelle *and* Mary could have been killed! But when I brought Mary back and told Jeannine about it, all she could say was, 'Oh, thank you.'"

"And you called CPS then?"

"No. This was before our falling out—you know why Jeannine and I had a falling out, right?"

"My guess is that you pointed out a flaw to her. That's usually the best way to get on her bad side," I said.

"Pretty much. Pete told me Jeannine had a prescription drug problem. I wasn't surprised in the least bit, but he begged me to say something to her, to try to get her to seek help. You can imagine how well *that* went over."

Probably about as well as the attempts to talk her out of the divorce, I thought.

"So much used to go on there, Pat, you have no idea…"

I probably should have paid a little more attention to what was going on around me. Unfortunately, as much as I regretted it, I couldn't change the past. I could only work for the future.

Elaine continued, "But I really earned my place on Jeannine's list the first time I called CPS. I was concerned about the mice in Shannon's room so I called to report the unsanitary living conditions, with children in the house."

My phone beeped in my ear.

"Hang on a second, Elaine? I have another call."

"Sure."

I pulled the phone away from my ear and checked the caller ID. My lawyer.

"Elaine, I'll have to call you back. It's my lawyer."

"No problem. Take care of yourself, Pat. Hang in there."

"Thanks. Bye."

"Bye."

I switched over to the other call. My new lawyer himself was on the other end. Not a secretary, assistant, paralegal or associate. Him. I was already far more satisfied with this guy than I'd been with my incompetent previous representation.

We had a new date for the emergency hearing: November 2, 2006.

CHAPTER EIGHTEEN

I sat with Shannon, silently praying again, begging God for a miracle. I watched the numbers on the little monitor that measured the pressure on her brain. The normal range, I had been told, was between five and ten. It was currently at thirty-four. The night before, it had leaped up to forty-seven and given us all quite a scare. Now, she was somewhat stable again. Up and down, up and down… I was never sure if I would still have my little girl the next day.

I reminded myself to keep positive, to think of Jeanna Giese, the fifteen-year-old girl in Wisconsin who had beat rabies—who was alive this day, two years later, after having been through exactly what Shannon went through, whose parents had sat by her side the way I was sitting with Shannon now. *They're probably the only ones who really understand*, I thought. I called every name in my cell phone and asked them to pray for my angel.

Finally, Jeannine arrived. Without sparing her a word or a glance, I went down to the cafeteria and grabbed something to eat. When I went back upstairs, what would the monitor read? Would it be up again? Would Shannon survive the day? Was she too far gone? Had those four days of Jeannine's "memory lapse" doomed my precious little girl? Or had she been doomed for months already?

I wished I could talk to the Gieses, find out if Jeanna had gone through the same ups and downs, twists and turns. As I finished up my soup and put the empty cracker wrappers in the Styrofoam cup, I looked down at my cell phone again.

I could call directory assistance and see if their number was listed—but how could I talk to people I didn't know? I wasn't even sure what I would say to them. How would I explain what I wanted? I didn't want to bother them. It might be a painful memory they'd rather not relive. What if they just wanted to be left alone?

But they would understand, I thought.

After opening and closing my phone several times, I sat up straight and dialed four-one-one.

"What city and state, please?"

"Milwaukee, Wisconsin."

"And what listing would you like?"

"Health Services."

"One moment, please."

Directory assistance connected me to Health Services in Milwaukee. A pleasant female voice picked up the phone.

"Health Services, Veronica speaking."

"Hi. My name is Pat Carroll. I…I was…" How could I begin? I cleared my throat and tried again. "I have a somewhat bizarre request for you."

"Yes?"

"I'm calling from Riley Children's Hospital in Indianapolis. My daughter has been diagnosed with rabies. I know there was a girl in Milwaukee who survived the disease."

"Jeanna Giese, yes," said Veronica.

I bent the plastic spoon in my hands. I was nervous, unsure of how exactly to phrase my request. "I just… I was wondering if I could leave my number with you to give to the Giese family. I would like to talk to them, to know more about things from their end. It's not important that I get in touch with them, I just would like to talk to someone who's been through it all."

"Hold for one moment, sir?"

"Sure."

As I was put on hold, I looked around the cafeteria. Other parents sat at the tables, some holding hands with spouses or significant others, some sitting beside children with brand new casts, some on cell phones looking distraught, and there, sitting by herself on the other end of the room, was a woman with a dazed look on her face. A full cup of coffee was in front of her, but she stared straight ahead, seeing nothing. There were dark circles under her bloodshot eyes, her cheeks were hollow and she looked thoroughly miserable, as if all of the light and happiness had been sucked out of her. No tears were spilling down her cheeks; it was as if she was all dried up. I knew—without asking, without overhearing anything—that she had just lost a child.

"Sir?" Veronica's voice pulled me back. I turned my gaze back to my empty soup cup.

"Yes?"

"Okay, let me get your phone number. I'll send the information along."

"Thank you."

I hung up from the call with Health Services, threw my empty soup cup in the trash and people-watched some more while I waited for my turn to sit beside Shannon.

The Giese family, as it turned out, were also the sort of people who reached out. They called me back within the hour. I spoke to Jeanna's mother, her father and Jeanna herself. All of them were very supportive and offered their stories to give me hope. They told me to call any time. They knew the fear of losing a child all too well.

I went back up to the PICU and sat watching the monitors again, talking to Shannon quietly, reassuring her—and myself—that everything would be all right. I told her about my conversation with the Gieses, prayed silently and tried not to think about what I would do if I lost her.

On Jeannine's next "shift," she showed up with more flowers, humming to herself as she found a place for them on the bedside table. She sat beside Shannon and began talking to her just loud enough for a passer-by to hear. I ignored her and left the PICU. Two hours later, when I returned, she was already gone. She did not come back at all that day.

Later that evening, one of the doctors on Dr. Costello's team, Dr. Avery, came in during rounds to check on things. He brought me a cup of coffee.

"Thank you."

"No problem. Thought you could use one of these," he said. He checked Shannon's IV, made a few notes on her chart and then turned back to me. "Does Shannon have a mom? I mean, did she pass away?"

"No. Her mother's still alive. We're just in the middle of a divorce."

"Oh. I've never seen her. Does she live far away?"

"No. She lives closer than I do."

"Oh." Dr. Avery sipped his own coffee, unsure of what to say.

I told him about the phone call I placed to Milwaukee Health Services and the Giese family's quick response.

"I wasn't sure if they'd call," I said, "but I figured it wouldn't hurt to try. And then, almost right away, my phone was ringing."

"A lot of times, families who have been through this offer their support to other people," Dr. Avery said. "Wouldn't you?"

"Of course," I said. "I most certainly would."

Every day for the next week, if I did not call the Giese family, they called me. I learned that Jeanna had had some symptoms that Shannon did not, and vice versa. Jeanna had experienced blurry vision, fainting spells and dizziness, while Shannon was vomiting and her tongue was swollen. Jeanna's parents, too, had experienced the roller coaster of hope and despair as the pressure on Jeanna's brain had increased and decreased. By Saturday, Mr. Giese told me that he and his family were planning on driving all the way to Indianapolis the following weekend.

"We'll treat you to lunch and sit and pray with you over Shannon. Sounds like you could use some company."

I was speechless. I opened and closed my mouth a few times, but no sound came out.

"Hello?" Mr. Giese said. "Pat? Did I lose you?"

"I'm here," I croaked into my cell phone. "Thank you. I really appreciate it."

When I went back upstairs, I was still warmed by the support. Something must have shown on my face, because as soon as I walked into the PICU, Juanita, one of the nurses, said, "What's going on? You have this stunned look on your face."

I told her about the Giese family's intended visit. Juanita smiled.

"They sound like good people," she said.

"Very good people. It'll be good to have them here. Especially since Dr. Costello leaves next week for Puerto Rico."

"Oh? He didn't tell you?"

"Tell me what?"

"I cancelled the trip," said Dr. Costello's voice from behind me. "I'm very concerned about Shannon's condition and I want to be here for any ups or downs."

I stared at him, my mouth hanging open. I burst into tears. After years of enduring Jeannine's selfishness, my faith in the goodness of people's hearts had been instantly restored. At that moment, the hospital wasn't so cold anymore.

Two days before the Giese family's expected arrival, Shannon took another horrible turn for the worse. One minute I was staring at her monitors, terrified by the number seventy-one on one screen's display, and the next, a nurse was calling for the doctors and I was ordered out of the cubicle. I took to pacing around the PICU, refusing to leave the area right outside the door. I was frantic.

Silently and furiously praying with everything I had, I begged God to see my little girl through this. I paced until my legs hurt. I sat down in one of the horrible plastic chairs, then stood up again. I could not sit still. Paced again. Sat again. Up again.

I don't remember Jeannine arriving. I know I filled her in somehow, but I don't remember the exact words I used. I'm not sure how long I did that. Twenty minutes? An hour? Several? I hadn't been watching the time.

When Dr. Costello emerged, the lines on his face had deepened. My blood ran cold.

"We're going to prepare her for an operation—essentially, to drill a hole in her head to release some of the pressure on her brain, but it does not look promising. I'm sorry. We're going to do all we can."

I called a Catholic priest to come and read Shannon her last rites. I wanted to be optimistic, but something told me that I had to be realistic as well. If this was going to be it, then I wanted my Shannon to be prepared.

And maybe it was a miracle, but she made it through the operation—my brave little girl clung to her life, refusing to let go. Dr. Costello and his team kept a close watch on her; they were not giving up, either. I left my cell phone charging on Shannon's bedside table, between two vases of flowers. I couldn't bring myself to call anyone. I didn't want to talk about it. I didn't want to leave her side.

By morning, the monitor measuring the pressure on her brain was close to the normal level. I dropped to my knees and thanked God, my hope for her recovery soaring.

Another miracle!

When the Gieses arrived the next day—Mr. and Mrs. Giese, Jeanna and Mr. Giese's sister—Shannon's pressure had crept up to the low twenties again, and she was more stable than she had been the past few days. Though I was always uncomfortable about leaving her side, when the Gieses got there, I went with them to the hospital's "family room" to talk. We pushed some tables together and sat down, facing each other at last.

Since it was lunchtime, I offered to have some pizzas delivered, but the Gieses declined. Instead, we just talked. They told me their story, and I told them Shannon's; they offered me as much advice as they could and I accepted it all wholeheartedly. Over the course of a few hours, we laughed and we cried, and we prayed together. At that point, this meeting was just what I'd needed.

The Gieses' presence at the hospital warmed my heart and renewed the hope I thought had died. After all, there was Jeanna, seventeen years old, alive and healthy, with a desire to go to college and study to be a veterinarian. She, too, had been in the coma while her family had sat by her side, unsure of what the next day would bring.

After they left, I went back up to the PICU, back to my chair at Shannon's bedside, and told Shannon all about the Giese family. I talked to her often, telling her everything would be all right, that I was proud of her. I felt that it helped both of us.

It was well past seven-thirty p.m., so Jeannine was no longer in the hospital. I looked around at the dozens of flower arrangements and teddy bears. She must have spent hundreds of dollars in the gift shop—Lord only knew where she got the money.

Mary and Kristine were, thankfully, still at my brother's house. The emergency hearing was only a week and a half away. I was sure I would gain full custody.

November second, I told myself. *Almost there.*

CHAPTER NINETEEN

On November 1, 2006, Shannon dipped lower than before. The pressure on her brain, already frighteningly high, was climbing rapidly. Dr. Costello and his team rushed in and out of her cubicle. Medical jargon whipped through the air, only snips of which I understood. I didn't care what each individual order or phrase meant. I knew only one thing: this wasn't good.

Late that night, one of the members of Dr. Costello's team, Dr. Katz, came out of Shannon's cubicle. We locked eyes and she began to walk toward me. I will never forget the look on her face.

Her jaw was set in a way that made her look confident in her judgment and abilities as a doctor, but her eyes were filled with the deepest sadness and regret. I knew then. I knew even before she said the words that I had dreaded since Shannon had been brought into the hospital.

"I'm sorry, Pat. The pressure is too high on her brain. There's too much brain damage. We've done all we can."

For a few seconds, I could not react. I just stared at her as if she had told someone else that their daughter was lost.

"She's hooked up to the ventilator for now. We would need your permission to take her off. Is there any family you would like to call? Have them come and say goodbye?"

Numbly, I nodded. Feeling crept back into me slowly. It started at my toes and fingertips—a slight tingling that shivered up my arms and legs and collided at my heart, twisting it, slicing through it and tearing it apart.

My knees felt like jelly. I staggered over to a plastic chair and slumped into it. My vision blurred and waved. I vaguely remember somebody offering me water, someone else asking me if I was all right. The room was suddenly hot. I felt like my face was burning with fever. Then I heard a horrible, soul-strangling cry. It took a moment to realize that it was coming from me.

The doctors called Jeannine and explained the situation. She immediately agreed, without hesitation, that it was best for Shannon to be taken off of life support. I called Peter, Mark and Barbara. The boys caught rides with friends, but Barbara was at a friend's house in Chicago. It took her a little longer to get there. When she arrived, she ran right into me, hugging me and sobbing into my shirt.

"No," she sobbed. "It's not fair! She doesn't deserve this! It's not fair, Dad, it's not fair!" She sobbed so hard she began to cough. I hugged her and calmed her down for an hour or so, and then we went inside and up to the PICU.

The five of us—Jeannine, Pete, Mark, Barbara and I—all stood together with the team of doctors. Dr. Costello and his team began to disconnect Shannon from the machine. I couldn't stay there. I couldn't watch them pull wires and disconnect tubes from my little girl—and I couldn't stand being near Jeannine while they did it.

Peter, Mark and Barbara couldn't watch, either. They joined me outside. We hugged, leaned on each other and cried together. I tried to hold my grief back, to just allow tears to trickle down my cheeks. My kids needed me. I could not let them down.

Jeannine stayed in the cubicle while they disconnected Shannon. I often wonder what went through her mind at that moment. Was she sorry? Did she realize what she had done? Or did she still claim that anything that happened was "God's will"?

When Shannon was off the ventilators, we went back into the room. She looked different—greenish. For the third and final time, she was read her last rites. I tried to concentrate on the prayers, but it was difficult to do so while being in such close proximity to Jeannine.

When the pastor was finished, I walked up to Shannon's bedside. I kissed her forehead and cheeks about five or six times, tears spilling uncontrollably from my eyes.

"I love you, Shannon," I whispered. "I'm sorry. I'm so sorry." I repeated this over and over.

Peter, Mark and Barbara each said goodbye to their sister, then left the room. They didn't want to watch Shannon as she died. I couldn't do it, either. I tried to stay, but watching her die was just too much for me to bear. Just before I left the room, I turned to Jeannine and looked her in the face for the first time all month.

"May God have mercy on your soul," I said.

I left the room.

Shannon passed away at five twenty-three a.m. on November 2, 2006.

Words cannot even begin to describe the despair and agony of losing a child. You feel as if your soul has been ripped out of you, slashed, burned, trampled and then devoured by a monster—and worse. The words "what if" and "if only" play in your head a thousand times a day, driving you insane. You want to curl up into a ball and fade into your own misery. You don't want to be cheered up. You don't want to move on. You want your child back…but it's too late.

My other children were the only things that kept me going, but it still wasn't easy. Shannon was my heart. I love all of my children, but Shannon and I shared a very close bond. She called me constantly. She could never wait to show me something she had learned. She was active, energetic and always the one to bring a ray of sunshine to anyone feeling low. She was beautiful, friendly and optimistic, and often took it upon herself to help out with Mary and Kristine.

She was her sisters' best friend. Mary and Kristine looked up to her, and Barbara was proud to have her follow in her footsteps. Pete and Mark adored her, as did anyone else who met her. She was such a great kid. I would never see her adolescent, teenage and woman years. I would never see her swim or do gymnastics again. I wouldn't be able to bring her to any more carnivals or batting cages, or take her on the go-carts. Mary and Kristine wouldn't have Shannon to teach them how to do cartwheels. Barbara wouldn't be able to teach her all about makeup or to talk about boyfriends. Pete and Mark wouldn't be able to play catch with her anymore or take her for a milkshake and fries. I would have one less daughter to walk down the aisle. We were robbed.

Why? Why did this happen to my little Shannon? I'd heard people spit out the old clichés, saying, "God only takes the best," and "It was God's will." God's will? I did not and would not buy that. Had it been leukemia, cancer or a rare heart disease, I think I would have had an easier time believing that and accepting her death. But not rabies. Not in this century. Not in this country. This could have been avoided, but for some unknown reason, Jeannine had decided not to seek medical attention for our daughter.

Did she not want anyone to question her parenting skills, or lack thereof? Did she not want anyone to check on their lifestyle? I would never know. I felt as if everything that fell from Jeannine's mouth was a lie.

Barbara told me shortly after Shannon passed away that over the summer, Shannon had told her that she'd wished she could live with me, but that she did not want to upset her mother. Shannon had had such a big heart, and such a sweet smile—one that I would only see again in pictures. It just wasn't the same.

I had several voicemails from Shannon saved from over the summer—I couldn't bring myself to delete them. I listened to them several times a day, just to hear her voice again. I couldn't believe I'd never hear her live voice again.

There was no doubt in my mind that the doctors at Riley had done absolutely everything they could. It had just been too late. I couldn't help but wonder how critical the four days when Jeannine had had her "memory lapse" were. What if…what if…if only…if only…

My angel, my heart, my little girl, my Shannon…in heaven now. A needless death from a seventeenth-century disease. I will never forgive Jeannine for that. Never.

There were several versions of the incident with the bat. The first was the version Jimmie Hackworth gave the local news station, where he knocked the bat off Shannon's arm. Then, there was Jeannine's version where she put peroxide on Shannon's arm after she'd been scratched by an unknown animal. And finally, Kristine's version that she told to Sara where Jimmie threw a blanket over Jeannine and Shannon when the bat landed on Shannon's arm. Which version was the truth? What was Jeannine trying to cover up?

At least Mary and Kristine were still safe with my brother. Charles, Sara and Jeannine's sister, Cassie, all agreed that it was the best place for them. They, too, were all outraged by Jeannine's memory lapse. I was grateful for their support. It helped remind me that I was not just being bitter and trying to place blame to cope with my loss. I had real cause for concern.

CHAPTER TWENTY

"I think you're making the right decision, Pat," Sara said as she helped me into my suit jacket. "Even though nobody else seems to think so."

Sara was, out of the whole family, the only one in favor of my bringing Mary and Kristine to Shannon's wake. We'd had a meeting the night before—with everyone from my side *and* Jeannine's in attendance (except Jeannine, of course)—and the unanimous vote had been that it was wrong to subject the small girls to that sort of grief. They were too young to understand what was going on; if they stayed home, they wouldn't even know what they were missing.

There was also another factor to consider, however: if I kept them away from Jeannine, who still had legal custody of the girls, it would be harder for her to get them back, and I had no plans to return them to her anytime soon. I was sure, at that point, that Jeannine was an unfit mother, that she did not properly care for the children and, in fact, fed them ideas that were detrimental to their well being. During the girls' stay with their aunt and uncle, they had said that their mother always told them not to talk to me about controversial events in their lives, or, "Dad will make trouble." That was why Shannon never told me about the bat bite. That was why Mary and Kristine had kept quiet, too.

I shook my head. "I know. I want Mary and Kristine to say

their goodbyes, to have a better understanding of…" My voice cracked, and I couldn't finish my sentence. Sara hugged me. I sobbed into her shoulder for a long while, and then broke away.

"Be strong, Pat. We're here for you."

I nodded and wiped my eyes. She handed me a tissue and brushed a piece of lint from my shoulder.

"All right. You're all set. We'll meet you there?"

I nodded again, and then gathered up Mary and Kristine, both already dressed in black. We got in my car and drove to the funeral home. We arrived at one o'clock p.m.—an hour before the service would start—so that Mary and Kristine could have a moment of privacy to say goodbye to their sister.

For once, Jeannine was early. As soon as I walked in the doors, she swooped out of nowhere, wearing a long, black evening gown and came directly over to the girls and me. Grabbing them by the hands, she didn't even look at me as she announced that she would take Mary and Kristine into another room to work on some pic-ture-board posters for Shannon, to keep them busy.

I shook my head and walked through the lobby and into the room where Shannon was laid out. I was the only one in there. Everyone else was either in the lobby or watching the scene Jeannine was making.

I approached Shannon's casket. She didn't look like herself, but like a life-sized doll, swollen and painted. I knelt before her and stayed there for several minutes, praying, silently talking to her, tears dripping from my cheeks onto my hands.

When I stood up, I noticed some of our old neighbors sitting in the second row. I greeted them, thanked them for coming and then excused myself from the room.

I went outside to get some fresh air and found most of Jeannine's family standing around in front of the funeral parlor: her brothers Jerry and Austin, sister Carrie, Uncle Austin, cousin Russ, Jerry's son, Jerry Jr., and daughter, Jolene, and his girlfriend Lisa. They were facing the street, standing there with their arms crossed, talking quietly among themselves. Looking past them, I could see what they were watching: a parade of police cars slowly patrolling the area.

I approached the group tentatively. "Hey, guys," I said. "What's going on?"

Jerry turned to look at me. "We all told you not to bring Mary and Kristine here. They won't understand what's going on. They should remember Shannon as she was—not how she looks in her coffin. You fucked up, Pat. You might as well say goodbye to them right now."

I couldn't think of anything to say back to him. What *could* I say? This was a no-win situation. I simply shook my head and turned to go back inside.

From what I later learned, while I went into the bathroom to splash some cold water on my face, two more squad cars showed up outside the funeral parlor and pulled up to the curb. An officer got out, approached Jeannine's family and told them he needed to speak with her. Austin went inside to retrieve her.

Once outside, Jeannine went up to the cop and launched into a speech about how her own family wouldn't let Shannon's "stepfather" pay his respects. With perfect timing, Jimmie himself showed up at that moment with a few of his cronies; he slithered up to Jeannine and took up the argument with her.

And that was just about when things really started to get out of control.

When Jolene heard Jeannine referring to Jimmie as Shannon's stepfather, she just lost it. "He is NOT the stepfather," she yelled at the police officer. "He's just the guy sleeping with her sick mother, and they're both responsible for Shannon's death! You need to arrest them—NOW!"

The rest of the officers got out of their cars then, seeing that things were about to escalate. One of them pointed a menacing finger in Jolene's face and told her, "*You'll* be arrested if you don't shut up."

As the rest of the family tried to hold Jolene back, Jeannine and Jimmie continued their meeting of the minds with the cop they'd been talking to earlier. Jeannine pulled out a stack of papers—the child custody agreement, which she just happened to have with her. Jolene saw this and quickly guessed what she was up to; she abandoned her argument with the police officer and ran straight over to her father and Lisa.

"We need to get the kids out of here now," she told them quickly.

Lisa nodded. "I'll go get the car and drive up to the back door. Meet you there."

Jolene composed herself and went inside the building, moving slowly and calmly so as not to raise anyone's suspicions. She found Mary and Kristine working on their posterboards for Shannon and told them to come with her—but Jeannine ran in right after her and said, with a huge smile on her face, "Oh, no. You're not taking them *anywhere*." Through the windows, Jolene could see all the cop cars outside, and police milling around everywhere.

At the same time, Lisa was pulling the car around, but found another cache of cops at the back door. It seemed like no one was getting out of that place—especially not with the kids.

At that point, I came out of the bathroom and was met by a police officer in the lobby. He explained to me that Jeannine had given him the custody papers and told him that I'd refused to return the girls after my parenting weekend. I tried to explain my side of the story, but the officer told me that it didn't matter. He had to call a judge to get a ruling on who would take the kids home that day, regardless of who the police might have thought the better parent was.

While we were trying to sort this out inside, outside, a stand-off was in the works. Jeannine's family and Jimmie's entourage were standing around, staring each other down. Jerry was exchanging dirty looks and obscene finger gestures with Jimmie; Uncle Austin was muttering to his nephew, Jerry Jr., that he wouldn't have any problem "taking down that punk hillbilly." Carrie, who had grown up on the South Side of Chicago and had a rough reputation, started screaming at Jimmie that it was his fault that Shannon had died. Even with her arm in a sling from a recent shoulder injury, she was raring to get into it with somebody.

Jimmie's sister then started shouting back at Carrie, and the chaos broke out all over again. Finally, after about five minutes of yelling, threatening and name-calling, the cops, who had been standing around watching the mayhem, told everyone that if they didn't quiet down, they'd be arrested.

Just as I finished up my conversation with the police officer in the lobby, the funeral director came storming in through the front door of the place. He'd just gone out and seen what was going on out there and marched right up to tell me that if the problems didn't stop immediately, he would close down the funeral. So, I went outside and told everyone to quiet down, and watched as the gangs broke themselves apart.

In this interim, a couple of things happened that again, I didn't learn about until later. One, Jolene pulled out her cell phone and called up a local TV news reporter who had been covering Shannon's story to tell her what was going on at the funeral parlor. Of course, the woman said that she'd be right over with a camera crew.

Second, a conversation occurred between Jerry, Austin, Uncle Austin and my son Mark, who'd been sitting on a brick planter outside the building, watching the whole thing go down. Uncle Austin asked Mark what had happened the night of the bat bite, and Mark said that he'd been there. He'd heard Shannon screaming around midnight—it woke him up and he went right into her room. He found Jimmie already there; Shannon was sitting up in bed, crying and telling him that a bat had flown in the window and bitten her on the arm.

"Don't worry," Jimmie had told her. "You'll be fine. See? There's no blood. It didn't bite you. Look, I knocked it off, and the cat will finish the job." Mark looked around and saw their cat scurrying out of the room with something in its mouth. He never saw a bat, but he sure heard the word used enough that night.

Uncle Austin asked if Jeannine had known about the bat, and Mark said that he didn't know—she'd never gotten up to check on Shannon that night, and Mark had never mentioned it to her afterwards. He figured that Jimmie had told her. Jimmie had also told him that it was "no big deal," that there were tons of bats in the area and that nobody ever died from contact with them.

Before long, the cops came back with the judge's decision, and they told me that although they knew that it probably wasn't the best way to go, they had to give Mary and Kristine to Jeannine. Triumphantly, Jeannine and her posse whisked the girls out of the funeral parlor; as they walked to her car, Jolene laid into her again.

"Murderer!" Jolene shouted. "You killed Shannon! No…no! You're going to kill one of them, too. You murderer!"

Jeannine put the kids in the car, and she and the jerk drove off without looking back.

Once she was gone, the TV news crews arrived with their cameras ready to roll, which drew the funeral director outside again. He pushed past everyone, approaching the news van driver and pointing back toward the street, shaking his head. I could hear the director's voice clearly, louder than anyone else's: "You can't stay here. This is a funeral home. Any interviews must be conducted off the property." The van pulled away, but parked again a moment later in the lot next door, where they set up to film. Jerry and Jolene both gave them interviews. Personally, I tried to stay as far away from the cameras as I could.

CHAPTER TWENTY-ONE

With Jeannine and her boyfriend gone, the funeral got underway rather peacefully. Hundreds of people came to pay their respects to Shannon—classmates, family, friends and even some of the staff from Riley. I stood in front of a maroon-upholstered armchair greeting mourners, dazed. Barbara, Mark and Pete stood with me. Barbara was furious with her mother and could not get the angry look off her face.

I was asked to give an interview with the local news team, but I still could not talk about what had happened. I wasn't ready. I just wanted to go home, curl up into a ball and sleep, so I could wake up from this nightmare.

Hours went by and still no sign of Jeannine. At around six-thirty p.m., I heard Barbara cluck her tongue. She looked at me and rolled her eyes.

Then I heard someone say, "What is she wearing? How can she think that's appropriate to wear to her own daughter's funeral?" I hadn't noticed Jeannine's clothes before, but now I looked at them and wondered as well what was going on there. It looked like she'd borrowed someone's old, ill-fitting prom dress.

But she wore it like she was on a fashion runway, gliding up past the mourners, a practiced plastic smile spread across her face. She stood on the other side of Barbara with a slightly dazed look. I did my best to ignore her. This was about Shannon. I would not give Jeannine the satisfaction of being the center of attention.

At eight o'clock, the minister began his eulogy. My brother and I took seats at the end of the front row, followed by Mark and Barbara. Jeannine sat on the other side of them, but not far enough away as I would have liked. As the service went on, she failed to shed a single tear for her departed daughter; in fact, I was pretty sure I caught her napping at one point. No one on either side of the family spoke to her the entire time.

And after the service, she was among the first to leave. As much as I wanted to go home and disappear, I didn't want to leave Shannon. After tonight, they would take her small body—as little as it looked like the bright, energetic, beautiful child she was—and cremate her. I knew I would never be able to look at her again. I wanted to stay with Shannon to the last possible minute.

A few family members lingered as the funeral home began to clear out. Barbara, Mark and Peter caught rides with friends back home. I stayed.

Cassie and her husband, Roger, were there, too. They had arrived just before the services had begun, and I hadn't had the chance to give them more than a quick hug as they'd gone up to pay their respects. With everyone clearing out, I was finally able to thank them for all of their help with Mary and Kristine.

"It was no trouble at all," Cassie assured me. "I wish I could have done more. When is your emergency hearing so you can get them back?"

"It was supposed to be on November second," I said, my voice cracking. I cleared my throat. "But obviously we...we couldn't make it."

"Do you have a new date yet?" Roger asked.

"No. I'm waiting for my lawyer to call me and tell me when it is."

"I heard about the fiasco earlier," Cassie said. "That, if nothing else, should help your case out. What exactly happened? I heard about three different versions already."

I filled Cassie in on the events from that afternoon. She shook her head.

"Unbelievable. Then Jeannine shows up late to the service, wearing that ridiculous dress. I think she was on something. Did you see her? Halfway through the eulogy, she was slumped in the armchair, her head drooped to one side. I half-expected her to start snoring in the middle of the service."

I was disgusted. Jeannine had reached a new low. This was her own daughter's wake. Throughout the two and a half hours she'd spent there, I never saw her shed a single tear. Nobody did.

The next day, I was pulled from sleep by the phone ringing. I tried to ignore it, to cling to my dream—Shannon was there, alive, playing, happy and healthy—but by the second ring, it had slipped from my grasp. It was gone. Groggily, I reached over to look at my cell phone's caller ID. Unknown caller. The phone rang again. I picked up the call.

"Hello?"

"Hi, Pat. I'm so sorry! Did I wake you?"

It took me a second to recognize the voice—Joan Rhodes, a friend from Portage, Indiana.

"It's all right. I had to get up anyway. What's going on?"

"Are Mary and Kristine with you?"

Wide awake, I sat straight up. "No. Why? What happened?"

"I saw Jeannine last night at Moon's Bar. Pat, this was like fifteen minutes after Shannon's services ended. I asked Jeannine where Mary and Kristine were, and she told me to mind my own business, and then she walked out. I was hoping they were with you."

"No. She took them with her yesterday after the wake. I'm trying, Joan. I really am." I told her all about the hearing no longer being deemed an emergency, then told her about the scene Jeannine created at the wake.

She clucked her tongue. "That's ridiculous. If anything, there's more of a danger now. Hang in there, Pat. You'll get them. Anyone can see you're the responsible parent here."

Hang in there. Stay strong. Keep your chin up. Words of encouragement are always appreciated, but then, they didn't do anything to help. Someone can say to do all these things, but when it all boils down, they don't know how hard it is to lose a child. If only Jeannine had put screens on Shannon's bedroom window. If only she had been brought to the hospital sooner. What if Jeannine had told the doctors about the bite to begin with? Would those four days have made enough of a difference?

If only...if only...what if... They wouldn't bring Shannon back.

The entire day went by in a blur. I hardly remember the funeral. Jeannine and I couldn't agree on a burial site, so in the end, Shannon was cremated and the ashes were split between the two of us.

Later that night, I found an article online about Shannon's wake. It reported on the police showing up, even going so far as to call it a "standoff." Both Jolene and Jerry were quoted in the article, and they took the opportunity to speak out on my behalf, expressing their outrage at the spectacle Jeannine had caused at her own daughter's funeral, and then mentioning that I was fighting for custody of Mary and Kristine.

It warmed me a little to see that Jerry had made a public statement in support of me. I read and reread his quotes, feeling more confident every second that when the custody hearing was rescheduled, there would be no doubt that Mary and Kristine belonged with me.

The article quoted Jimmie saying that he was the one who had knocked the bad off Shannon's arm and ended by noting that Jeannine could not be reached for comment on the situation. *Naturally*, I thought. *She can't be reached for anything, unless it has something to do with herself.*

The Saturday following the wake, the pastor at a church in Tippecanoe was kind enough to give a memorial service in honor of Shannon. I walked into the church at ten a.m., an hour before the services were scheduled to start.

I went by myself—I felt I needed some time alone on the drive to think, listen to the radio and get lost in the highway. As soon as I walked through the church doors, I felt a lump rising in my throat. Jeannine had set up a table the night before with several framed pictures of Shannon—playing baseball, swimming, school portraits and a few random, candid shots. I stood back from the table and stared at my daughter's smiling face, wishing with all my might that I could hug her again.

In the center of the table was a large picture frame with a glare coming off of the glass. I took a step closer so I could get a clear view of the picture, and I recoiled.

It was an eight-by-ten glamour shot of Jeannine.

"Mr. Carroll?"

I turned to see the pastor standing behind me. I shook his hand and thanked him for holding the service.

"You're welcome," he said.

"I'm sorry," I said, gesturing to the photo of Jeannine. "I just don't think this one here is very appropriate."

He didn't think so, either. He told me that he would make sure it was off the table before the service began.

"How are you doing?" he asked.

I shrugged. "Depressed all the time."

He offered me a few words of encouragement—words that I had heard countless times since Shannon had first gone into the hospital—and prayers. I thanked him again and then sat down in one of the front pews, to pray silently before the service began.

At eleven o'clock, when the service was set to begin, the pastor approached me and asked if I had seen Jeannine yet. I shook my head. He waited five minutes. Then ten. Finally, at eleven-fifteen, he began the half-hour-long service without her.

A few people spoke at the service, but I couldn't bring myself to go up there. I knew I couldn't talk about Shannon without getting choked up. In the middle of one old neighbor's story, I heard the church doors open. I didn't even have to turn around to know it was Jeannine. I glanced down at my watch. Eleven thirty-five. She was a half hour late for her own daughter's memorial service.

A few days after Shannon's service, Jeannine showed up at the school that Shannon had attended in the morning. She was a mess—hair unwashed, wearing pajamas as clothing, babbling incoherently. She somehow got into Shannon's fifth grade class and kind of overtook the place, standing in the front of the room and rambling on to the children about Shannon and what had happened.

Well, of course, this scared the kids—and the teacher, too, who ran to the principal's office for help. The principal came in and escorted Jeannine back outside the school and told her that she shouldn't be there talking to the kids in the state she was in. Jeannine, I'm sure, was offended and belligerent, but wandered away from the school and from what I understand, did not give them any more trouble.

A mother of one of Shannon's classmates called me to let me know what had happened that morning, and I got right on the phone to the principal. Unfortunately, she was in Shannon's former classroom, talking to the kids Jeannine had terrified, assuring them that everything was okay and explaining that Shannon's mother was just going through a rough time or something. Since I couldn't get a straight story from anyone about what was going on, I decided to call the Bourbon police and ask them to go check on my kids—which they did, and everything with them was okay. The whole thing was just such a strange incident; I was glad that for once, Jeannine did not escalate the situation into a full-blown scene. She left before causing any real problems at the school.

CHAPTER TWENTY-TWO

While channel surfing one particularly depressing afternoon, I caught a little blurb on a disease called Munchausen Syndrome on a mid-afternoon talk show. It got me to sit up in my chair. Munchausen patients often go to great lengths to feign, simulate, worsen or self-induce diseases or psychological trauma in order to attract sympathy and attention. They are addicted to hospitals and are known to have unnecessary operations and procedures in order to investigate or correct their imagined illnesses.

"I'll be damned," I said. It was Jeannine to a T.

Jeannine's behavior was devoid of all rationale and any consideration for anyone but herself. She was manipulative, knew how to tell people exactly what they wanted to hear and knew when and how to push people away when they came too close to figuring her out. Was she really that selfish? I didn't understand how anyone, particularly a mother, could be that way.

I had been married to Jeannine for long enough to know that while she did have her quirks, she was not always so deranged. She was not always addicted to methadone and other prescription painkillers. She wasn't always so irresponsible, so reckless, so far fallen. I, along with many members of her family, believed that she may have had this serious mental illness known as Munchausen Syndrome.

Unlike those with hypochondria, who truly believe that they have a particular disease, Munchausen patients know that they are exaggerating. They have an extensive knowledge of rare and unusual diseases, their symptoms and causes, and sometimes even go as far as to cause the disease they are in the process of simulating.

They like being the patient. They relish in the attention, sympathy, treatment and care from medical personnel in particular, but they are reluctant to have that medical personnel meet with family, friends or prior healthcare providers. They often have predictable relapses as soon as there is any sign of "improvement" after a procedure.

They keep people at arm's length so no one can figure them out. They are aware of what they're doing but can't stop themselves. While their actions are conscious, the motivation behind those actions is not—it is out of their control.

Learning about this disease, I thought I'd finally figured Jeannine out.

She used to be close with her family. Then, all of a sudden, she'd begun to push them away, especially when they'd questioned her frequent doctor visits or her prescription drug addiction. She had always been willing and eager to go under the knife, and she knew the ins and outs of the medical care system as if she had set it up herself. She constantly complained of back pain, and occasionally, other "symptoms" would show up. She'd get herself checked out for certain and then feign pain in the appropriate places at the appropriate times.

When Peter had told Jeannine that he'd been diagnosed with ADD (Attention Deficit Disorder), she'd asked him what kind of medication he was on and to describe, in detail, the affect the prescriptions had taken on him and his symptoms. She'd announced that she thought she, too, had ADD and wanted to be tested for it. She'd behaved as if her life depended on having continuous medical illnesses.

There was no doubt in my mind that Jeannine qualified as a Munchausen patient. What infuriated me to no end was the fact that with all this knowledge of disease and hospitals and Medicare,

Jeannine could not be bothered to act when Shannon had been bitten by a bat. Was it a self-image thing? That had always been way too important to Jeannine. Had she not wanted people to know that something like this had happened on her watch? Had she been drunk or high at the time and afraid of coming across as a bad parent? Did she not want people asking why she didn't bring Shannon to the hospital the night it happened? Why had she kept quiet when asked if Shannon had been bitten or scratched by any wild animals? Was her appearance more important than her daughter's life? Because I don't believe for a second that Jeannine truly forgot about the incident.

I doubt I'll ever know what really happened or what went on in Jeannine's head. And to be perfectly honest, it doesn't matter. I can't forgive her. Her neglect, her selfishness, cost me one of the most precious things in my life. She claimed to be depressed all the time, but she did not shed a single tear at Shannon's wake. She didn't blame herself at all for our daughter's death. She didn't see herself as an irresponsible parent—but even Jimmie, the ex-con, the bane of my existence, had told her she was an unfit mother. Mark had overheard him say this during an argument with Jeannine and had told Pete about it; Pete had passed the information on to me.

I never thought I would agree with that poor excuse of a man. But I wanted custody of my children—all of them. And Jeannine needed some serious help.

I often wonder—and it drives me mad—if Jeannine had spread her sick little world out onto Shannon.

Before divorce had ever been discussed, Jeannine and Elaine had been sitting in the backyard, reading a book on palmistry for fun. Straight-faced, emotionless, Jeannine had announced that Shannon's lifeline was very short and she probably wouldn't make it to adulthood. At that point, Elaine had changed the subject, shocked that Jeannine could even *say* that about her own child.

Elaine had told me about that incident just to clue me in on Jeannine's strange behavior. Now, it haunted me.

Jeannine always had to be right. Did she deliberately not seek medical attention, making Shannon a victim of Munchausen Syndrome by Proxy? I just didn't understand how any parent could "forget" about something as traumatic and significant as Jimmie and Jeannine claimed the bat attack had been.

My fury had no words. As depressed as I was over the loss of Shannon, I was becoming more worried sick for Mary and Kristine. I'd already lost one child. I would not be able to bear it if anything happened to any of the others.

CHAPTER TWENTY-THREE

I expected my emergency hearing to be postponed. I expected that a week or two after the funeral, Mary and Kristine would be in my custody and all of my children would be out of harm's way. I expected the court system to do what was best for the safety and well-being of my children. Instead, the hearing was cancelled and rescheduled.

Apparently, since Shannon had passed away, the way they saw it, there was no longer a child in immediate danger; there was no longer an "emergency." The earliest court date I could get was January 29—two months away.

"Are you kidding me?" I shouted into my phone when my lawyer's secretary told me this. Tears of rage poured down my cheeks. "No emergency? *No emergency?* My daughter is *dead!* Do they want to wait until something happens to another one of my kids?"

"I'm sorry, Pat," my lawyer's secretary said. She was remarkably patient with me. "We're trying our best to get the hearing moved up, but for now, it's at the end of January."

I couldn't believe what I was hearing. Two months. Two months with Mary and Kristine in Jeannine's hands. I couldn't wait that long. I felt, and still feel, that Shannon would be alive today if it weren't for Jeannine's selfish and bizarre behavior.

"I can't believe this! How could the courts not see this as an emergency? How could this not grab their attention? Anyone's attention?"

"I'm sorry, Pat. I don't know what to tell you."

I paced around my living room, my eyes darting from the window to the framed pictures on the walls, to the door, back to the pictures again. "Well... I..." I pinched between my eyes and took a deep breath. I felt no calmer than I had before. "What if I just didn't bring the girls back after my parenting weekend?"

"That would be considered kidnapping."

"Good! If I were arrested, do you think that would get the state of Indiana's attention? Get the media involved! Let them know that she's an unfit mother and my children should be anywhere else!"

"Pat, I cannot, will not and do not advise you to do that."

I knew I was yelling at the wrong person, so I ended the phone conversation with a quick apology and then slumped on the couch, willing myself to wake up from this nightmare. I listened to Shannon's voicemails again, cried for an hour and then began to search the want ads in the newspaper. I had to keep going, taking it one day at a time.

About a week after Shannon passed away, I started writing everything down. All my thoughts, everything that had happened—I noted everything I could think of, anything that might be of use when we finally got to court. I wanted to be as prepared as possible, to build the best case I could against Jeannine as an unfit mother.

The more I wrote, the more I thought about everything that had happened and the angrier and angrier I got. I could not let Jeannine get away with what she'd done; whether she wanted to admit it or not, she had caused the death of our daughter. I had to do something about it.

My first call was to Child Protective Services, where I spoke with a woman named Kim Lehman. At the time, I didn't even know what I was looking for, and Kim listened to me talk until I figured it out; I just needed someone who understood what I was going through, and she seemed to do just that.

To follow up on my complaints that Jeannine was not taking adequate care of our children, Kim arranged to interview her and Jimmie at their house. Unfortunately, Kim had to schedule an appointment with Jeannine for this interview so when she got there on the designated day, Jeannine had already had a chance to scrub the place until it sparkled, put food in the refrigerator, bathe the kids and put them in presentable clothing. She'd had time to get her shit together, and so Kim—and the police officers who had accompanied her—did not get a true picture of how my kids were living.

This whole thing was—and still is—just unbelievable to me. When CPS schedules appointments with people they're investigating, it gives the parents ample time to get their houses, themselves and their kids in order. Wouldn't you think that CPS might like to see how things *really* are in the environment in question? If they did, they would show up unannounced, and at key times—like during the morning rush, when parents should be helping their kids get ready for school, or late at night, when the kids should be in bed. This is how they treat people on parole—the officers can show up any time, day or night, to get a clear picture of how the person is really living. Why is it different for CPS?

If they had made an unannounced visit to Jeannine's house— even just one visit—I'm sure that they would have had a different view of her mothering abilities. In the morning, she would have been asleep while the kids were getting themselves ready for school (or not, if they decided they did not want to go). Late at night, they may have found the kids asleep anywhere but in their beds, and Jeannine downstairs partying with her degenerate boyfriend and who knows who else.

Why is this system so screwed up? How hard would it be for someone—anyone—at Child Protective Services to say, "I think I need to drop by this house without telling them, because I think they're hiding something from me"? I know they've all had their suspicions. It's time for them to start conducting surprise visits to see how they really live.

Kim's report stated that the children lived under "bare minimum" standards, but that nothing illegal was going on. I was disappointed, frustrated again, but I couldn't blame Kim for just reporting on what she saw during that one staged visit.

So, I next called the Bourbon police department and asked what kind of report *they* had filed about Shannon's death—and if they had found any liability on her mother's part. "No," I was told, "we didn't fill one out."

"Well, *would* you write a report?" I asked, hoping that they could still do something.

"No," I was told again. "As far as we're concerned, the case is done."

I sighed and ran my hand through my hair. My frustration just grew and grew; I wondered if any satisfaction would ever come of this. "I'm not happy," I finally told the officer. "Where can I go to do something about this?"

I swore that I heard him chuckle. "I don't care of you go to the FBI or the CIA. We're done with it."

I slammed down the phone, hoping that the noise hurt his ear on the other end of the line, then I slammed a six pack and smoked a joint.

The next day, I called the state police, where I was taken a little more seriously. Sergeant Lynn Johnson was assigned to my case and over the course of the next ten months, conducted an extremely thorough investigation into what had caused Shannon's death—and who, if anyone, was responsible for it. I gave her names of everyone I could think of who might have information, and she interviewed every last one of them—even though many avoided her because they had their own criminal backgrounds to worry about and didn't want to get involved.

After interviewing Jeannine and Jimmie, Sgt. Johnson told me that she had a gut feeling that both of them were no-good liars, and that something *had* happened with them that had something to do with Shannon. She had gotten one person, someone close to the family, to admit that Jeannine had told them about the bat bite, but there really was no proof; it would be this person's word against Jeannine's, and how could anyone determine who was telling the truth? That was how the law would look at it, anyway. This information, unfortunately, had to stay "off the record."

In the end, Sgt. Johnson said that she would like to see charges filed against Jeannine and Jimmie, but was afraid that after she turned in her report, it would go nowhere. There just wasn't enough hard evidence, and the case wasn't prosecutable. A girl getting bitten by a bat wasn't a crime.

But she handed in the report anyway, and we're still hoping that something will come of it.

On November 17, 2006, I woke up bright and early, ready to pick up Mary and Kristine for my parenting weekend. Finally! The weeks since Shannon's wake had been absolute torture. On top of the agony of having lost one of my babies, I was worried sick that something would happen to one of the others while they were in Jeannine's care. I was more than ready to go pick up Mary and Kristine for the weekend—and even better, the following weekend was Thanksgiving, and it was my turn to have them for the holiday.

Maybe I can convince Jeannine to leave them with me for the whole week, too, I thought. I knew she would put up a fight, but if I phrased it right, maybe, just maybe, she could be reasoned with.

As I put on my coat, the phone rang. Mark and Barbara were still sleeping, so I grabbed it. It was my lawyer.

"Oh, hi," I said. "Listen, I'm about to head out the door to pick up my kids. Can I call you later?"

"That's what I'm calling about."

Jeannine had contacted her lawyer regarding my decision to leave Mary and Kristine with my brother and his wife following my parenting weekend, rather than return them to her neighbor, who I did not know. Jeannine wasn't stupid. She was manipulative and vindictive, but never stupid. She knew I had no desire to return Mary and Kristine to her care at all.

She was now using that incident as a stepping stone.

"Before you see your children, I need you to come down to my office and sign a restraining order she filed."

"Sign a what? I can't stop by. I have to go get my kids."

"That's the thing, Pat, you have to sign this document first, or you will not be permitted to see your children."

I sighed. "I'll be there in ten minutes."

I hung up the phone, stood there for a moment and then slammed my fist down on the kitchen table. "Goddamn it!" All I wanted to do was pick up my children. Now I had even more of a delay.

The quick drive to my lawyer's office calmed me down a little bit, but not much. My lawyer saw me right away and handed me the restraining order that I was supposed to sign. I read it over thoroughly.

It stated that I was not permitted to "exercise any parenting time" with my children that was "inconsistent with Indiana Parenting Guidelines" unless it was put in writing and signed by both Jeannine and myself, or the children would be turned over to Jeannine's custody without a hearing.

Indiana Parenting Guidelines were reasonable enough. They were mostly what should be no-brainer regulations for divorced parents—one parent not interfering with the child's correspondence with the other, giving ample notice of a moving date, giving the other parent up-to-date phone numbers and addresses—but they also outlined specific times in which the children had to be returned to a custodial parent.

According to the restraining order, I was responsible for picking up and dropping off my children during parenting weekends, or I forfeited my weekend. That was nothing new. Jeannine had long since stopped meeting me halfway. I had been making the hundred-twenty-mile trek—each way—from Oak Lawn to Bourbon for years.

One thing that stood out to me in the order was the clause that stated that neither Jeannine nor I were permitted to discuss blame for Shannon's death with any of our children. I suspected this was the real reason she had filed for the restraining order in the first place—so I could not warn my girls to tell me if something happened.

It was degrading, but essentially, I didn't have any choice but to sign. If I didn't, I'd have lost any and all rights to even visit Mary and Kristine, and they would have been left in harm's way.

I scribbled my signature on the dotted line and left to go get my kids.

Jeannine could not be reasoned with. She demanded that I return Mary and Kristine to her at the end of the weekend and then pick them up again on Wednesday night for Thanksgiving. The three days between the weekend and the holiday were painfully long. I was sick with worry. I called several times a day to check on the girls, sometimes asking Barbara or Mark to do so in my stead.

Wednesday was exceptionally long. I could not pick them up until the evening, so for most of the morning and afternoon, I habitually glanced at clocks and watches every two minutes, wishing that time would go by faster.

After waiting all day, I decided to leave to pick up the kids at three-thirty p.m., just in case there was extra traffic for the holiday—and there was. The hundred and twenty miles from Oak Lawn to Tippecanoe had never seemed longer. There were traffic jams everywhere. On the side streets, every car in front of me seemed to be puttering along at a snail's pace. Traffic lights were not in my favor. At every stop sign, it seemed as though cars would never stop streaming past to allow me to make the turn. At long last, I was only a mile away from Jeannine's house.

I called her. There was no answer. Annoyed, I called again. No answer. I called again.

Jeannine picked up.

"Hello?" She was clearly annoyed at something.

"I'll be there in two minutes. Please have the girls ready."

"Oh. I forgot to tell you. We moved."

I gritted my teeth.

"You moved again."

"Yeah."

"Without my knowledge."

"Yeah. I just forgot to tell you."

I pulled over to the side of the road. "Why didn't you tell me last weekend? Or weeks ago? How long have you known about this?"

"I just forgot."

"You seem to be forgetting a lot of important things lately," I said.

"Don't start, Pat." Jeannine warned.

"Fine. Give me the new address."

"I don't know it."

"You don't know your own goddamn address?"

"No, I don't," Jeannine snapped. "We just moved here the other day."

"Well can you tell me how to *get* there?"

They hadn't moved far, but Jeannine's directions took me down the wrong street, and I had to call her two more times to get to the right house. Each time I got off the phone with her, I asked her to have the girls ready. I had no desire to go to the front door and confront her, and she did not want me anywhere near her. This had been our arrangement for a long time.

The road was dark, with no streetlights. In the glow of my headlights, I could see that the front lawn of Jeannine's new residence was more dirt than grass and was littered with a few crushed beer cans. The siding of the house was in disrepair and the whole thing was in need of—bare minimum—a paint job. There was even a "no trespassing" sign nailed onto the front porch. I wondered what the conditions inside were, but knew I would not be welcomed to inspect it.

What looked like an old bed sheet hung over one of the windows in lieu of a curtain, and I saw it pushed aside, and Mary's face appear. She cupped her hands against the glass and peered out and then ran back, letting the bed sheet cover the window again.

I waited. Two minutes. Five minutes. I shut my car off. Ten minutes. "Come on, Jeannine," I muttered.

Fifteen minutes. Seventeen. Fuming, I honked the horn.

At twenty minutes, the door opened and Mary and Kristine came running out. I got out of the car and opened the trunk so they could put their backpacks in and saw that Kristine's jeans were too small. Mary, whose coat was unzipped, wore a sweatshirt with a hole in the shoulder. I would have to take them shopping on Friday to get them new clothes.

I helped the girls buckle themselves in and started the car back up again. "Ready to go?" I asked. "Did you both go to the bathroom?"

They told me they had. I pulled away from Jeannine's house and began to retrace my steps to get to the highway.

"I'm hungry," Mary said.

"Did you have dinner?" I asked, glancing in the rearview mirror. Mary shook her head.

"What did Mommy make?"

"Nothing."

I sighed. "All right. We'll stop on the way, okay?"

There were several fast food places on the way to the highway. The first place we saw was Taco Bell. A lump rose in my throat. Although Kristine and Mary were cheering for it, I could not bring myself to turn in. That was Shannon's favorite. I could still see the beaming smile on her face when I would pull in to one. I could still hear her voice ordering the same thing every time. I wasn't ready. I went to McDonald's instead.

As Mary and Kristine ate their Happy Meals, I felt the knot of worry loosen in my stomach. I had them for the weekend. They were safe, for now.

In one day, Jeannine had violated several of the Indiana Parenting Guidelines, including not giving me ample notice for a move, not having the kids ready to go and letting them wear ill-fitting, torn clothing.

On the following Monday, I called my lawyer to let him know all of this, and he said that we might as well wait to address it at our court date on January 29. I agreed, but had a feeling that she would never face any consequences for it; on the other hand, if I had done the same thing, I would have lost my parenting time. The courts tended to favor the mother—even when she was unfit—and so I pretty much wrote this incident off as another on the long list of things Jeannine would never have to pay for.

My case was not the only instance where a father's rights were glossed over. In *Summers v. Summers*, a custody case in Gordon County, Georgia, the father is currently struggling for equal parenting rights. According to his Website, 5050parents.com, his ex-wife, while not a threat to his daughter's life like Jeannine, has deliberately kept his daughter from him, cutting off all contact and denying him access to his own child. The courts have ignored this.

He does not ask for primary custody; he asks *not* to have secondary custody. He wants equal parenting, but it is denied him. His divorce, like mine, was bitter and the custody battle even more so. Not only was the presiding judge his ex's lawyer's former law partner, but he was told that his job was not flexible enough to allow him to spend more time with his daughter.

That case, however, involves two competent adults, whereas there are many, specifically in Indiana, where an unfit mother is still favored over a fit and loving father. The Indiana Civil Rights Council, a fathers' rights activist group, began with a divorce. The mother had been proven to be verbally and physically abusive to her three children, while the father was involved with them in every way—soccer coach, Cub Scout leader, girls' softball booster and all-around volunteer. Even so, the mother was awarded primary custody of the children.

For a while, the father ended up acting as the custodial parent, but when he petitioned the courts for legal custody, they retaliated by taking away his extra parenting time and nearly doubling his child support. He was arrested and jailed under false accusations four times, resulting in over two years of his life being ripped away from him for no real or good reason.

I did not want to end up like this father and so set about doing whatever I could to lay a good groundwork for myself—something that would give me a leg to stand on when I finally got my day in court.

To build this foundation, my brother-in-law Jerry and I wrote letters, starting in January 2007, to just about every person we could think of who might be able to make a difference: members of the Bourbon Town Council, the governor of Indiana, the Indiana state police, Child Protective Services, the judge who was presiding over our case—hell, I even sent one off to the Dr. Phil show. Jerry wrote letters on my behalf, as did his daughter, Jolene, Jeannine's sister, Cassie, and my son, Peter. Their words characterized Jeannine as the deplorable, dangerous woman she was, and practically begged for help.

We sent them all off one at a time, via certified U.S. mail or Federal Express, hoping and praying that somehow, they would make a difference in the outcome of my case. But our letters may as well have been messages in bottles from a deserted island in the middle of the ocean. To this day, we have never received a single response from anyone we wrote to. Copies of these letters can be found on www.rabiesmom.com.

CHAPTER TWENTY-FOUR

The bias in the court system, unfortunately, worked against me as well. After two months of frustration and worry, January 29, 2007 finally arrived.

I stood there in court, in my suit, sweating a little. This was far too important for me not to feel nervous. Jeannine was wearing appropriate, professional clothing; neither of us acknowledged the other's presence. My lawyer had thought it best if I did not even look at her. I agreed with him. Just thinking about her made my blood boil.

Our divorce was not even final yet. The process had been prolonged by nonstop debates—we couldn't reach an agreement on anything, especially when it came to the kids.

Our lawyers approached the bench and spoke with the judge. Evidence was presented—testimonials, photographs, payment records, hospital records and so on. I sat there for hours, keeping my eyes fixed on my lawyer as he argued for me. When he was finished, Jeannine's lawyer said his piece.

I expected a quick decision. I expected to walk out of there that day with custody of Mary and Kristine. But I was learning that the courts never did what I expected.

"There is contradictory testimony here," said the judge. "We're going to have to have a full hearing with fifteen character witnesses for both sides."

My heart fell into my stomach like a rock, and sat there. Another delay! How much longer would I have to worry?

A few weeks, I told myself. *It will just be a few more weeks.*

But a few more weeks was too long. Every second of every day that my daughters were in her care twisted my insides in knots.

Our lawyers and the judge reviewed their calendars for a while. When they returned, my lawyer's mouth was creased into a frown. He did not have good news for me.

"The first date they have available is August seventh."

"*August?*" I cried. "Are you kidding me?"

"Shh! Keep your voice down, Pat."

I rubbed my eyes with the heels of my hands for a while, unable to believe what I was hearing. August! Half a year away!

"I can't wait that long," I whispered.

"I'm going to try my best to get it pushed up," my lawyer assured me, "but for now, that's the best we can do. We're going to try to get things finalized for your divorce on that day, too. In the meantime, try to make a mental list of witnesses on your behalf."

I didn't have to think hard. Faces leaped into my mind's eye: Charles, Sara, Jerry, Jolene, Cassie, Austin, Pete, Mark, Barbara, Elaine—anyone who was at the wake would be able to attest to Jeannine's outlandish behavior. I could think of a score of people off the top of my head.

I buried my head in my hands. "Is there no justice?" I asked.

"There is, Pat," my lawyer assured me. "We just have to wait for it."

More waiting.

But what if it's too late by then? I thought.

Because we never actually got to have a hearing at the January 29 court date, the information regarding Jeannine's moving without telling me was never brought to light. Honestly, I'd been so blown away by the further delay that I hadn't even thought to mention it to my lawyer, but I guessed that even if I had, he would have just told me that I'd have to wait until August to address it anyway. By then, I wondered, would it even really matter? I went home and got plastered. I deserved it.

I started a new full-time job with a local automobile transport company, and I wasn't about to give the courts any excuse to side with Jeannine. A few days into it, I received a call from Barbara on February ninth, toward the end of the day.

"Hi, Dad."

"Hi, sweetheart. Everything okay?"

"Yeah. I was just wondering if you had Mom's phone number."

"Yeah, I do. Why?"

Barbara had not spoken to her mother since Shannon's wake. She was absolutely furious at her behavior and wanted nothing to do with her.

"It's her birthday. I just thought…well, maybe I should call her. She *is* my mother."

"All right. Hang on a sec." I pulled my cell phone away from my ear and fished through my address book for the most recent number Jeannine had given me to get in contact with her. When I found it, I rattled it off to Barbara.

"Thanks, Dad," she said.

"Honey, just…be careful. You know how your mother can get."

"Yeah, I know. I will. Thanks."

Barbara hung up the phone and took a deep breath. She stared for a moment at the phone number she had written down.

She's your mother. It's her birthday. Be the better person, Barbara. You can do this, she thought.

She dialed the number and listened. One ring. Two rings. Three. Four. Just as she was about to hang up, Jeannine picked up the phone.

"Hello?"

She sounded groggy, as if she'd just woken up.

"Hi, Mom. Happy birthday."

"Oh, hi, Barbara, honey. Thank you. How are you?"

For a little while, Barbara and her mother had an awkward, almost forced conversation. They talked about what was going on at Barbara's school for a minute, about cheerleading and gymnastics, and then Jeannine quickly turned the focus of the conversation to herself.

"I don't know how you do it with gymnastics, sweetie. You have a lot of energy."

"I guess," Barbara said.

"I'm so tired today. I don't know why."

"You sound like you just woke up."

"I did. I was lying down."

"What time did you wake up this morning?"

"Around eleven-thirty," Jeannine said.

Barbara rolled her eyes.

Jeannine continued, "My back has been hurting me so badly lately…"

Barbara listened to Jeannine piss and moan about her back pain, headaches and various other symptoms of the latest condition she thought she might have.

"I called my doctor and tried to get him to up my prescription. It's just not working anymore. So I have to go in for more tests next week."

"You do? On what?"

"They're going to do some blood work and some other tests."

"Oh," said Barbara. There was a moment of silence. Barbara cleared her throat and then asked, "So…are you happy, Mom?"

A pause. "And what is that supposed to mean?"

"What do you mean? I was just asking if you were happy."

"Am I happy that Shannon is dead? Is that what you're asking me?" Jeannine snapped.

"No! I—"

"Well, I'm not! I'm depressed all the time! How's that for you, Barbara?"

Barbara raised her voice back. "I was just asking if you were happy!"

"You know what, Barbara? I'm going to go now. I can't believe you would imply such a thing!"

"What are you talking about, Mom? I just wanted to know if you were happy! That's why you left Dad, isn't it? That's why you tore our family apart and went off with Sam and Jimmie, isn't it?"

"Goodbye, Barbara."

Click.

Barbara slammed the phone down on the receiver, even angrier than before. She stormed to her room, screamed into her pillow, then called up some friends to vent.

Children, especially those as young as Mary and Kristine were, trust their parents implicitly—and should be able to. They don't know that a parent should wake up with them. They don't fully understand that not seeking medical attention could kill them. They don't know right from wrong yet. It is a parent's job to teach them.

Mary, Kristine and Shannon had dutifully kept quiet about Shannon's bat bite because they were told that, "Dad will make trouble." Indeed, I would have "made trouble," and I believe that Shannon would be alive today if I had. Children trust their parents to know what is best. Mary and Kristine were too young to know that they could not trust their mother.

Jeannine tried to be the "cool mom," the one who was friends with her kids, but in trying to do so, she had foregone all parenting whatsoever. I know for a fact that she had allowed Peter and his underage friends to drink in our house. She had let Mark drive without a license. She let Barbara get her belly button pierced at fourteen. She never told them to clean up after themselves or help out around the house, and neither did I. They did what they wanted and got away with it. They became lazy.

Yet when push came to shove, Jeannine's priority was herself. She missed Mark's and Barbara's birthdays. She ignored Pete's pleas for her to get herself some help. She hardly noticed when Mary or Kristine snuck away from her. She allowed Shannon's bat bite to go unchecked and pretended to know nothing when asked if Shannon had been bitten by any wild animals. She manipulated the police and CPS every time the neighbors called them to come to the house.

It was nine-thirty a.m. and already, my day was crazy. Work was swamped—it was just before the Fourth of July and a short work-week was always a busy one. I had already decided to work through my lunch break, but that did not go quite as I'd planned it. I received a phone call from my lawyer at around ten o'clock.

"Pat, I have good news."

"They moved the hearing up?" I asked, hope rising.

"No. I'm sorry. Not *that* good news. But something to give you a little confidence."

Nothing was good enough beyond having the hearing moved up. It was still a month away.

"What happened?" I asked.

"Jeannine's lawyer resigned as of June twenty-first. The necessary paperwork has already been submitted and approved by the court."

"Why did he quit?"

"He claims it's because of nonpayment. I can only guess that he finally saw our side of the story."

It was good news, but it set off alarm bells in my head.

"So what is this going to do for the hearing?" I asked. "It's going to be pushed back, isn't it? Give her new lawyer some time to get up to speed."

"There isn't an attorney out there who would take this case," he said.

"What about a public defender?" After all I had been through,

I had little faith in the system. The only way I could not be surprised was to be pessimistic.

"There are none in civil cases. Jeannine has to be there. If she asks for a continuance, I'm going to object to it. She's had more than enough time to prepare her defense. In my opinion, she has less than a two-percent chance to keep the kids."

The news gave me hope, but the hearing was still a month away.

On July 13, 2007, I came across an article on Foxnews.com that made me restless for my trial date. A woman in Texas was imprisoned for criminal negligence after her two-year-old son fell down the stairwell of her apartment building and she failed to bring him to the hospital. She put a Popsicle on his head injury, using it as an ice pack, and put him to bed. When the father later arrived, the little boy was "unresponsive." His head injury proved fatal, and the mother was promptly arrested.

A wave of emotions crashed over me. At first I was angry. How was it that this woman was arrested for neglect and Jeannine not only ran free, but still had custody of Mary and Kristine? Why was my emergency hearing canceled because of Shannon's death? Why wasn't Jeannine arrested for neglect? Was it the state of Indiana? The individual judge? Jeannine's manipulative abilities? Maybe I was in denial, and it really was all my fault.

I paced around my living room, rubbing my temples, muttering expletives that I hoped would never come out of my children's mouths. After fuming about the injustice of the legal system for a good twenty minutes, I looked at the article from a different angle. This could possibly set a precedent for my upcoming hearing. I had to think positively.

I slumped back on the couch and ran my hands over my face, and then slammed my beer.

"Twenty-five more days," I whispered to myself. "Just twenty-five more days."

CHAPTER TWENTY-FIVE

On August 3, 2007, Jeannine and the moron showed up at the office of Jack Rosen, my lawyer, for their depositions. They had originally shown up on August 1—as they had been subpoenaed to do—but had refused to give any testimony that day, as they were not represented by a lawyer of their own at the time. This was also the reason why I was never deposed—because they didn't have a lawyer to do it.

Since our court date was only six days away at that point, my lawyer filed motions to force Jeannine and Jimmie to be deposed. Since Jeannine was a principle in the case, the motion was granted: she had to show up and give her deposition, or she'd be held in contempt of court.

A friend of mine tried to cheer me up by suggesting that I start a pool among family and friends, taking bets on just how late Jeannine would show up.

"You could take ten percent," he said. I appreciated his efforts, but I was too nervous for that. I couldn't bear the thought of another delay.

Jimmie was the first one to be deposed. He was sworn in to tell the truth, and then the questioning began.

"Okay," Jack, my lawyer, said, shuffling papers in front of him. "Would you state your name for the record, please?"

"Jimmie Hackworth."

"Your date of birth, please?"

"April 17, 1960."

"Sir, where did you graduate from high school?"

He folded his hands and placed them in his lap. "I didn't. I only went to ninth grade."

Jack questioned him on how he'd known Sam, how he'd come to work at my house and Sam's unfortunate demise.

"Were you present?" Jack asked, regarding the supposed suicide.

"Yes, I was." Jimmie dragged out these three words for full effect, his voice baleful, his eyes looking weary.

"Had he made any indication to you that he was going to do something that erratic?"

"No, sir. He was just shooting through the house. Rochester police have all this. He was shooting through the house. I took the gun away from him several times. Then he shot beside the couch, almost shot me, and then he just kicked the gun up under his chin and blowed his brains out. No rhyme or reason." He leaned forward in his chair and looked up at my lawyer, eyebrows raised. "I have a lot of personal stress about this."

The story seemed rehearsed and practiced, but that wasn't something that Jack had to be concerned about at the time. This court date was about my kids' safety and well-being primarily, and second, about divorcing myself from Jeannine. Whether or not this miscreant had killed his new friend unfortunately wasn't any of our concern.

So, back and forth they went. Jack asked where Jimmie lived, what his specific trade was, whether or not he had a driver's license, how much jail time he'd done for being a "habitual traffic violator," and about the various places he had lived with Jeannine and my children—Bourbon, Tippecanoe and then finally, back to Bourbon again.

"So then yourself, Jeannine, and Shannon, Mary and Kristine all lived there?" my lawyer inquired.

"Yes, we did."

Jack then asked him if Jeannine was on any medication.

"She used to be on methadone," Jimmie reported. "I don't know if she still takes it or not. I think Klonopin, something for her legs. She gets restless leg syndrome."

"Does she still take methadone?"

"I don't know if she still does. She used to."

"She used to up until when? How long ago?"

"It's been several months."

"Who prescribed that for her? Do you know?"

"No…some doctor in Fort Wayne…a pain clinic."

"Was that for her back? Legs? Neck?"

"For her back and her—whatever else is wrong with her."

Jeannine would put herself on medication for a cramp in her finger, this made me think, *but she never brought my Shannon to the hospital.*

Jack then said, "Okay. I want to draw your attention to June of 2006, a little over a year back, with Shannon. What is your recollection of Shannon being bitten by a bat, a bird, an insect or whatever?"

"I was asleep," Jimmie said. "I think Terri lived there with us then. And I came home from work the next day. And Jeannine was telling me something about a bird or something and a scratch."

What a liar. How many different versions of this story would there be when all was said and done? Which one of his thousand tales were true?

"And, see, I work ten- to fourteen-hour days," Jimmie continued. "I came home, I ate, I showered, I went to bed. I'm up at three in the morning every day."

Jack nodded in that mysterious way that attorneys have—the way that makes you think you might have said something completely damning. Giving no indication either way, he simply went on. "So you came home and Jeannine told you about a bird and a scratch?"

"Yeah. I didn't think nothin' about it. You know, like I say. Work, come home, go to bed—eat, shower, go to bed."

"Okay," Jack said. "Did you ever talk to Shannon about it?"

"No, I didn't."

"Did you ever tell any newspapers, magazines, or television stations that—"

"I think I did, but I was coming down with sarcoidosis at the time."

"Coming down with what?" my lawyer asked.

"Sarcoidosis. It's a lung disease. I was delusional. I have proof."

Jack, ever the professional, did not change his expression or his direction. "And did you tell them a different story about what happened?"

"Probably."

"Do you recall what story you told them?"

"Actually, I don't. Everything—I got sick. I was in the hospital at the University of Indianapolis at the same time Shannon was. In the emergency ward, they had me checked in under the name Dr. House—I mean, Mr. House—because there was a lot of conflict going on with Pat Carroll."

The notion that I would cause problems with Jimmie just then, especially when he was checked into a completely different hospital, was absurd. My primary concern at the time had been, of course, my daughter. I hadn't cared where he'd gone or what he'd done, just as long as he wasn't at Riley to give me a hard time while my little girl was fighting a losing battle for her life.

"What hospital were you checked into?" Jack asked Jimmie, continuing with the deposition.

"University of Indianapolis."

"When was that?"

"I'm thinking October."

"Okay. October of 2006?"

"Yeah."

"And you were checked into the hospital for what? I'm sorry."

"Sarcoidosis. S-C-A-R-I-D-O-S-I-C-A. It's a weird name. It's a rare disease."

"And what does it allegedly do?"

"It hits the major organs of your body. Boy, it struck my lungs. When I got to the hospital, I had forty percent oxygen in one lung, thirty in the other. I was delusional. I didn't know anyone."

Didn't know anyone? He sure knew *me* well enough when he was giving me the finger in the PICU!

"So it's your recollection," Jack went on, "that if you talked to anybody in the press, you were delusional at the time and didn't know what you were telling them?"

"Yes, sir."

"So if you told the press that in fact, Shannon called you into the room and you saw a bat on her arm and knocked it off, that didn't happen?"

"No, sir."

"So you're delusional in September, and you don't remember any of this stuff?"

"Not—just bits and skips. I'm still bad with it. Just bits and skips of things is all I remember."

"How long were you in the hospital?"

"Seven days in intensive care."

"Were you released from the hospital before or after Shannon died?"

"Before."

"Do you recall if the interviews you gave to newspapers were before or after Shannon died?"

"They were before."

"Did the Department of Children and Family Services or the Welfare Department interview you?"

"Yes, they did."

"And did the state police interview you?"

"Yes, they did."

My lawyer nodded again and flipped over to a new page of his legal pad. "Are you on any medication now?" he continued.

"No," Jimmie said, and then paused. "Prozac. Forgot about that." He reached into his back pocket and pulled out a folded piece of paper. "Here's a list of the medications I take."

My lawyer took the list and looked it over, but said nothing.

"And add Vistaril to that," the jerk said.

A short recess was called to make copies of the list, which was subsequently admitted into evidence. Then, the questioning continued.

"Okay." Jack looked at his notes, flipped through a couple of pages in front of him and then continued. "At the house where you live with Jeannine and the two children now, do you receive any type of state aid, or does she?"

"Food stamps," Jimmie answered. "Or, did."

My lawyer looked at him blankly. "Have they stopped now?"

"Yes."

"Was Jeannine getting them up through July of this year?"

Jimmie shrugged. "I don't know. I honestly don't."

Again, another lawyer nod, and a change of subject. "Have you had any work in the last two months?"

"Yes, I have, at Graphix Unlimited in Bremen."

"Do you work full-time now?"

"No, I don't."

"So that job at Graphix doesn't exist now?"

"Doesn't exist." Jimmie seemed to be getting bored with this line of questioning.

"When was the last time you worked there?"

"Two weeks ago."

"How long had you worked there?"

"A couple months."

"Before you worked there, where had you worked?"

Jimmie sat up straighter in his seat. "I had done some remodeling. I had help from my family. I've been sick all winter. But I done some remodeling up in Portage."

"Okay," Jack said in his usual, unimpressed tone of voice, and then immediately switched topics again. "How would you describe your relationship with Mary and Kristine?"

"I have a good relationship with them," said Jimmie. "I love them. They love me."

"Did you attend Shannon's funeral here in town?"

"No. I was advised not to by the police officers."

"Did you attend the memorial service? I believe it was in Lafayette."

"It was in Tippecanoe. Yes, I did. So did her father. He was welcome."

"Did you and Jeannine arrive on time for that?"

"Yes, we did."

"Okay," my lawyer said at last. "I have no other questions."

CHAPTER TWENTY-SIX

There was another recess, and then Jeannine sat down for her deposition. She looked skinnier than ever, wearing black pants and a tight, button-down shirt. Her hair was stringy. She looked like nothing more than a lying, manipulative drug addict.

Jeannine swore to tell the truth, though it was doubtful that she would. In her own twisted little world, the universe revolved around her and she truly believed all of her own lies. She sat there smugly, holding a stack of papers in front of her and looking ready to take on the world, sure, as always, that she was the only one in the room who was right.

Jack began by going over the marital assets for purposes of the divorce. Immediately, Jeannine was abrasive and argumentative, and it all took a lot longer than it had to. They went over assets, debts, personal property, her bankruptcy, money she thought I owed her, things we had to split up. Jeannine nitpicked every detail she could and of course, tried to make herself look like the poor victim at every turn.

Thankfully, my lawyer knew better than to take her bait. He waded through all of the mundane details of our life together, boiling it down to who got what car and who had rights to the pension and stocks. And then, finally, he got on to the topic that meant more to me than anything else in the world at that moment in time.

"Let's talk about what happened with Shannon," he began. "Was there some type of incident in June of 2006 where Shannon was bit?"

"No."

"Okay. Did Shannon receive any type of an animal bite in June?"

"Not that I know of."

"Did you ever tell a next-door neighbor that Shannon was bitten by a bat?"

"No."

Her ability to lie about her own daughter like that—repeatedly, straight-faced, unrepentant—was a little scary.

"Did Jimmie ever tell you that he, in fact, had taken a bat off Shannon's arm?"

"Never."

How could she? I thought. *How could she sit there and lie under oath without a second thought?*

"Okay," my lawyer continued. "Tell me what, in your opinion, occurred or did not occur in June, which resulted in Shannon having a scratch on her arm."

"I was sleeping. Terri Fellman was living with me. She was sitting at my dining room table, reading a book."

"Who is Terri?"

"Terri Fellman. She's a girl who was having problems with her husband. She stayed with me. She ended up helping me. She helped me out with the kids."

"So she was living with you in June of 2006, then?"

"Yeah, because I had an injection in my back. So it was right after June eleventh, which is Peter's birthday, too. So that's how I know when she got there. And then Gulf Stream closed on the Fourth of July. So I know that as a landmark. And then September thirtieth is when Shannon's symptoms—"

"I want to go back to June," Jack interjected calmly, as though not even listening to her incoherent babbling.

"Okay. Now I'm going back. So sometime at the end of June, Shannon came downstairs, and Terri was sitting at the end of the table, reading. The kids were all in bed, sleeping. I was in bed, sleeping. Jimmie was in bed, sleeping.

"I got a knock on my bedroom door, and I got up and answered it. And Shannon was there, and she said—she was kind of disoriented, and she was saying, 'I think something flew in through Mark's window. I think something was on my arm. I don't know what happened. Something really scared me.' I thought she was talking in her sleep.

"So I went out and saw Terri sitting there. I said, 'What's up?' And she said, 'She came down and she just said she was really scared, and I tried to help her out, but she wanted her mom. So she knocked on your door.' I turned to Shannon and said, 'Well, honey, what's the matter? Are you walking in your sleep? Are you *talking* in your sleep? Do you have to go to the bathroom?'

And she said, 'No, I think that there might have been something on my arm. And I got really scared, so I came down and I knocked on your door.'

"See, Mark had the small room upstairs and the girls had the large one. It was really hot up there and he always took the screen out of his window, thinking he got more air in that way. And Shannon was always saying, 'Something is going to fly in through that window. You know I'm scared of birds. Tell him to put that screen back in the window. The mosquitoes are getting in, and what if a bird gets in?'

"So I went upstairs. Terri went up with me. I turned on the light. We brought Shannon up. The girls—Mary and Kristine—were still sleeping. I looked around, but saw nothing. The room was clean. Shannon was real neat, liked her things in order.

"And she was going, 'But I think something scratched me.' And I said, 'Well, did you scratch yourself today while you were playing? Did you scratch yourself moving around in your bed? Were you having a nightmare?'

"'I don't know, Mom,' she said. 'I think maybe a bird flew in the window. I thought that I felt something, but I don't know.'

"I never thought it was anything but a bird," Jeannine commented, shaking her head yet again. "I wish... I wish I did. But I didn't."

"Okay. What did you do then?"

Jeannine jumped as if she'd been pulled back to reality. "Well, there was no blood. She had a tiny scratch, just—not even like—there was no blood. She had a little scratch. And I said, 'Well, if something did scratch you, you watch for infection. Put peroxide on it, put a Band-aid on it and keep an eye out to see if it swells up and turns red.' That's what I did. That's what I did. Found no bat."

"Okay," Jack said, though I wish he had asked her about a thousand more questions—all of them hard and unforgiving: *Why didn't you disinfect it yourself? How could you let a little girl be responsible for her own medical care? Why didn't you take her to a doctor, at least, if not the hospital? Why didn't you take our daughter seriously?*

"So, Jimmie didn't tell you that he had taken a bat off of her arm?" he asked instead.

"No, no. He came home from work that night, and we would always go over the account of the day. And I had this cat that was driving me crazy. And I—I had my gall bladder taken out. I had an injection in my back that went bad and I was having a hard time even walking."

Jeannine could not go a minute without turning the discussion toward herself and her problems. This was supposed to be about what had happened to Shannon, not about Jeannine's laundry list of supposed ailments, but she was so selfish. She only wanted to solicit sympathy for her health issues, not get to the bottom of what had really caused her young daughter's death.

"This cat," Jeannine continued, "did not meow when it wanted to get in the house. It did not wait until somebody let it in.

It took out my screen window and jumped in, and it pounced on my stomach with whatever half-dead animal of the day it had in its mouth. I wanted the cat gone. I was sick of it."

Jack paused. "What does this have to do with anything?" he asked.

Jeannine shot him a little look that said, *How dare you talk that way to me*. But then she shook it off, and went on with whatever the point of her story was. "What this has to do with it is, some days after this happened, Jimmie came home from work, you know. The cat had another animal, that kind of thing, you know. I'm sick and tired of the cat. The cat has to go."

She sounded flustered, as though she'd forgotten what her story was supposed to be.

"I understand that," Jack told her. "So you're telling us that Jimmie was at work that morning when—"

"He was sleeping," Jeannine said flatly.

"Okay. So when did you first tell Jimmie about this bird or whatever?"

"The next day, when he came home from work. He said, 'Was Shannon knocking on our door last night?' I said, 'Yeah. She woke up and she thought something was on her arm.'

"He went up and searched the room, but found nothing there. He said, 'I don't see nothin' up here either.' I said, 'There's nothing up there. I don't know if she was having a dream or what.'

"So, then some days later, my son Mark came home from work, and he came into the house right before me. And he said, 'Oh, look at this.' I said, 'What is that?' He was pointing at the cat, who had some sort of mutilated animal in its paws. All chewed up. Yucky, yucky. I took it away from the cat. I said, 'That is the ugliest thing I've seen in my life. Get rid of it." Mark threw it away. End of conversation.

"So the way that this whole story was put together is, some friends of mine needed a baby-sitter for their daughter. They had come by, and the wife said, 'Hey, are you going to be home? We have to go to Plymouth. We'll be gone about an hour and a half.' I said, 'Yeah, I'm busy with everything I'm doing in the house.' And we just started talking and you know, one conversation led to—and I'm like, 'Do you know anyone who wants a cat? I have this cat that's—'"

"Is this sometime in July, or…?" my lawyer asked, interrupting her long stream of nonsense.

"This is probably some time in July or August. Someone who wants a cat. I can't stand this cat."

Again, all about her—about how *she* didn't want the cat. It was unbelievable how she could turn even the most inane story into something all about herself.

"These friends asked me how I liked living in the house. They used to live there in that same house, years back. And I said, 'Well, maybe you can give me a hint, because I've got the dog and I've got the cat and I've bombed the house. I can't get rid of the fleas. I don't understand it.'"

Jeannine went on for several minutes about the conversation she had with her friends about fleas—where they came from, how to get rid of them—and then again returned to the cat and his dead animals and how much she hated it. She rambled like she was drunk and just enjoying the sound of her own voice.

Finally, Jack broke in. "Go on with the conversation. So you're talking to them and then what?"

"They said, 'Well, isn't it really hot upstairs? That's what we did not like about the house. The kids slept downstairs because it was so hot upstairs.' I said, 'Yeah, it's hot up there. As a matter of fact, Mark keeps the screen off his window. Shannon is always complaining that she's paranoid about the screen. And they're always fighting about mosquitoes and flies, and she's scared a bird is going to come in. As a matter of fact, one night, she thought it did. I went up there and looked around, but I didn't see anything.'

"Well, my friends pieced together this conversation about the cat with the animal conversation. Cat, bat—bat cat, you know."

"Your friends did?"

"They were saying what could have happened to Shannon, and they pieced it together. I didn't. They did."

"What did they piece together?"

"Different conversations that we had that day, in the course of about twenty minutes, while they were in their car, asking me if I could keep an eye on their daughter. You know, how do I like living in the house, it's hot upstairs…"

"So they put this together. Who did they tell this to then?"

"The woman from Bourbon Family Medicine. I had brought Shannon to see her on Tuesday and for an X-ray on Wednesday. I called—"

"What is this?" my lawyer interrupted, apparently having a little trouble following what Jeannine was talking about—as most people did.

"For her arm."

"In September?"

"In September, when her symptoms began, when I had to go to the school and get her when she—"

"Before we get to that, wait. So then you have this conversation with your friends and apparently, at the time, they don't say anything about a bat to you at all, do they?"

"No."

"Okay, so you treat the wounded arm?"

"It's not *wounded*. It's a scratch."

"So you treat the scratch and it goes away."

"Yeah. No red, no nothing. My nails made a—my nails would make a bigger scratch than what she had."

I thought, *What kind of wound would a bat make? What kind of mark did Jeannine think a bird would make?*

"So, then sometime, Pat had the children for visitation. Is that correct?"

"That's correct."

"Okay. And while she was on visitation with him, did Shannon call you and say she felt like she had the flu or something?"

"Yeah, she did. She called me on Saturday."

"Saturday, at the end of September?"

"Yes. I believe it was the thirtieth."

"Did she come back on Sunday?"

"Uh-huh."

"Okay. Then what happened?"

"She was complaining about her arm," Jeannine said, "and she was just complaining that she was tired."

"The arm she was complaining about, was that where the scratch was?"

"The arm—" Jeannine began, then stopped, and appeared to be trying to get her facts straight in her mind. "I go over it all the time in my head," she admitted, and I thought, *Well, that much is obvious.*

Finally, she continued: "In her room, the way her bed was, the way that she did it… It was her left arm." I wondered if anyone—including herself—had any idea what she was talking about. "The arm that she was complaining about—when she came home from her dad's, we thought it was a pulled muscle because they had gone swimming, and Mark was saying, 'She pulled a muscle. There's nothing wrong with her. I'm sore, too.'"

"Okay," my lawyer answered blankly.

"That was her right arm that was sore," Jeannine then offered. "Because I sent a note to school that she—you know, to give her a break on writing. She pulled a muscle on the weekend with her dad at the hotel."

Again, all this solicited from Jack was an "okay."

Jeannine continued, on a roll now, unfazed by my lawyer's lack of reaction. "I did her homework for her Monday—she gave me the answers and I wrote them down. Her arm was hurting her. When you first get a sore muscle, it's going to get more sore, and then it's going to get better.

"Well, then on Tuesday, the nurse from school called and said that Shannon had thrown up on the floor in her classroom. So I went and I picked her up. And her arm was getting more sore. And so I brought her to the doctor."

Jack paused in his questioning of Jeannine. "When you're saying 'sore,'" he asked, "what do you mean?"

"Hurts," Jeannine said a little too loudly; remember, she never liked being questioned on anything she said. "She was really complaining, to the point where I brought her to the doctor." She made it sound as though Shannon were a whiny baby, nagging at her mother until she had to finally give in and—gee, what a great idea!—get her some medical attention.

"She had thrown up," Jeannine recounted. "She wasn't feeling good. And you know, she'd had a bit of an upset stomach lately. I didn't know if it was a nervous stomach or what. Pete had asthma. Mary had, you know, her allergies. Me, in turn, the same way. Shannon was having a difficult time when she was running, exerting herself. I told the doctor all of this."

Jeannine paused then, as if gathering her thoughts again. "Okay," she went on at last. "Let's deal with one thing at a time. Let's deal with the arm. So they did the range of motion tests and everything. And I was telling Shannon, you know, that this happened to her on Saturday, Sunday, Monday, Tuesday. That it was a sore muscle. Something had to have happened somewhere in there, because it was going down her arm. That sounded like nerve impingement to me.

"The nurse practitioner ordered an X-ray of Shannon's arm," Jeannine continued. "Also, of the collarbone and a chest X-ray. And she said that Shannon had thrush in her mouth, and gave her Nystatin. And I said, 'Well, how about her upset stomach?' And that was when the nurse gave her Pepcid—or did she wait to give her that until Thursday?"

Jeannine put a finger up to her lips, her brows knit as though she were really pondering her own question. "I'm not sure because

I brought her on Tuesday. I brought her Wednesday to the hospital for the X-rays. I brought her back to the doctor on Friday because I knew the weekend was coming, and she wasn't getting any better."

The level of detail that Jeannine could recall was amazing—names of medications, tests ordered, days on which they were done. How could she keep that all in her mind, but "forget" to mention, while Shannon was in the hospital, that our daughter had been bitten by a bat—or scratched by a bird, or whatever she wanted to claim that it had been?

"It was like Shannon had gotten the flu," Jeannine went on, "and was just not getting better. Her arm was not getting better. I brought her back to the doctor on Friday and they said, you know, 'Just give her as much fluids as you can. Crackers, fluids, whatever you can get down her.'

"Saturday—and she just had such a hard time sleeping." I loved how Jeannine started to say one thing, and then always switched to something else. It was a clear sign how disjointed her mind really was. "She slept on the couch all week long. And Saturday when I got up, I said, 'Honey, you know, I have been a mom for twenty-something years now, and I'm thinking I'm not qualified to take care of you anymore. I'm thinking you need IV treatment.'

"'No, Mom, no, Mom, no!'" Jeannine practically shouted, in a high-pitched voice that was supposed to be an imitation of my ten-year-old Shannon. "Well, by Saturday afternoon, it was, you know, 'Babe, we're getting you together and we're taking you to the hospital because Mom can't do this.'"

If only she had admitted that a week earlier.

"Which hospital did she go to?" my lawyer asked.

"Plymouth, St. Joseph Regional. Brought her to the emergency room. Told them everything that had—you know, she called me Saturday." Again, that fractured form of storytelling that showed Jeannine's truly disconnected mind. Maybe she'd been about to say something incriminating about the night that Shannon had been scratched—or bitten, or whatever—and then realized it, and so turned the subject to something else. "She was not feeling well. She had been swimming all weekend. She came home with her arm sore. They did an X-ray. Her arm was getting worse, up to the collarbone."

"I'm assuming the X-rays were negative, then?" Jack asked, completely ignoring Jeannine's repetitive story.

"X-rays were negative, X-rays were negative. And so they had her on IV treatment, and they were just kind of—the doctor was out of town, and it was a different doctor. Friday night—let's see. Friday night." Again, a finger went up to her lip, and her eyes glossed over a little bit. Was she trying to recall the past, or wondering what her next lie should be?

"Saturday, she was in the hospital, and she was just getting sicker, and she didn't have a good nurse. As a matter of fact, I had left the hospital to go get Shannon new pajamas, slippers and panties, so I could wash her and change her clothes, and so I could get away from the nurse. She was saying that she thought that if Shannon would sit up, she could swallow, and that her breathing was clear. And I was saying, 'She sounds like she's drowning. Her breathing does not sound clear to me. It sounds like she has pneumonia.'"

Jeannine actually stopped here to roll her eyes a little bit before proceeding. "'Breathing is clear, *Mom*,' that nurse said. She was very rude to me."

Of course, that was the most shocking part of the entire situation to Jeannine.

"I left," she went on. "I went and got Shannon's stuff. Jimmie's sister and brother-in-law came, and they spent time with Shannon, kept an eye on her while I left. We spent the night in the hospital. I slept in the bed with Shannon. And I left to get away from this nurse, because she was just not giving my daughter good care at all."

So, her daughter was not getting good care, Jeannine thought, and her solution was to *leave the hospital*? To get away from the "rude" nurse, instead of staying and advocating for her seriously ill daughter? Unbelievable.

"And I got back," she continued, apparently seeing nothing wrong with her previous statement at all. "And Jimmie's sister said, 'Jeannine, she had one of those *fits* that she was having. She couldn't breathe. She couldn't swallow. I went and got the nurse and the nurse is just blowing it off.' And I said, 'Okay. This isn't working out real well. So would you do me a favor, nurse, so that I can sleep tonight?'" Jeannine went at this with such drama, with all the belief, it seemed, that *she* was the one who was really getting the bad treatment in that situation.

"'Would you please call the doctor and have the doctor come and check my daughter again? Because she's not doing well. And you're telling me that this is good and her lungs are clear, but she can't swallow. Her speech is getting bad. You know, I need to be able to sleep tonight, and she is miserable and she's getting worse. I want a doctor to come see her.'"

And the Academy Award goes to… It was surprising that Jeannine hadn't risen out of her chair and banged her fist on the table in front of her. This had truly been an admirable performance.

"Three minutes later, the doctor comes on the floor. She talks to me, goes to Shannon and then leaves the room. I follow behind her. She's on the telephone, and I'm standing there listening to her. She hangs up the phone. She says, 'Okay, Mom. I called up to Indianapolis, to Riley's Hospital and I called up to Fort Wayne, to another hospital, and I'm talking to specialists in regards to what is going on with Shannon neurologically. Obviously, there's more going on than we can do here, because we don't have the equipment and we need an MRI. That arm is not getting any better, and you have an MRI scheduled, but that's not until next week, and we can't wait. And she's having a hard time breathing. So I'm thinking that it would be best if we transfer her to Riley's Hospital, in case she needs to be intubated.'"

She said all this practically without taking a breath. Again, there was her amazing recollection of details and facts, compared to that first night at Riley's Hospital.

"Well, I know what this word means," she continues. "My mother was intubated. So I said, 'Do you think she would need life support?' And the doctor said, 'No, I'm not saying that she's going to need it. I'm saying that as a precaution, we need these tests in case we need assistance in breathing, but I do not foresee that. That's the best place for her, because they have everybody there that she would possibly need, and we will get these tests—bam, bam, bam.'

"Okay, fine,' I told her. 'You got to call her dad.'"

That's right, leave it up to the complete stranger to inform me that my daughter has been stricken with a mysterious, life-threatening illness. Don't bother to tell me yourself that my Shannon might have to have a tube put down her throat to help her breathe! Let me hear it from someone who doesn't even know me, or you, or Shannon. That seems like the most logical thing to do.

"So, this is late Saturday night, then?" asked my lawyer, continuing with Jeannine's deposition.

"This is Saturday, about six o'clock."

"Okay. So then you called Pat?"

"I called Pat, and he knew she was in the hospital. I had told him—he knew she was sick all week. And I let him know what was going on. And I said, 'Would you please call her dad and explain to him what is going on?'"

"So you had the nurse or the doctor call?" my lawyer asked.

"That doctor." Nice answer. She didn't even know the doctor's name. "So she could explain, because I'm kind of freaking out here. But she's got me reassured, and it all happened really fast.

"So she called Pat, and she told him exactly what she told me.

I was standing right there. He said, 'Let me talk to her mom.' And to me, he said, 'Do you think I should head out?'

"I said, 'Well, it's a really long drive for you,' though it turned out to be shorter from Chicago than it was from my place. And I said, 'They're saying they're going to do a spinal tap and they're going to do these tests and they're going to do an EEG on her brain and they're going to do an MRI on her arm. You know, if you want to hold tight, they're saying they're going to do all these things really quick. I'll let you know as soon as they start to get some feedback.'"

"They were going to transport Shannon to Riley's to do all the tests, right?" Jack interjected.

Jeannine nodded. "As a precaution."

"I understand. You were talking to Pat about going to meet you at Riley's?"

"Yeah. He wanted to know if he should. And I said, 'Let us get there, let them get the stuff going, and then I'll call you and let you know what starts to come back in.'"

"Did they transport her right away, that Saturday?"

"They transported her right away, immediately. And we weren't in the door five minutes at Riley's, and she was intubated. Five minutes."

"So you called Pat then and told him to come to Riley's?"

"I didn't have to call him. He came rushing in while they were putting her on life support."

Did she really think that I would sit around at home, waiting for a call about some stupid test results? I'd been in my car and on the highway within minutes of hanging up from our phone conversation.

"They had pulled the curtain, and I stood outside, and I just had my hair in my hands. I was banging my head against the wall. I didn't even know what to do.

"And then he came flying in. And I said, 'Don't go in there. Don't go in there. You can't go in there. Stop.' And he just started yelling at me—'That's my daughter. It's my daughter. Fuck you.'

And I was telling him, 'Who wants to go in and see their daughter put on life support? You don't even know what's happening.' I was just trying to stop him."

"Did he go in and see her?"

Jeannine nodded. "He went in, and they brought him back out."

"Did the doctors then interview you and him together?"

"No. No, never."

Unbelievable! I thought. *How could she not remember standing there—me and her and the doctor at Riley—talking about Shannon's condition and answering questions about whether or not she'd had any contact with animals?*

Jack even seemed a little bit incredulous. "The doctors never interviewed you and him together, asking about whether she had been exposed to any type of bites or whether or not she had been exposed to swimming in any polluted waters or around new construction or anything?"

"New construction, no. Woods, mosquitoes, stuff like that."

"Did they ask—"

"They asked me everything."

"Okay."

"They were everywhere."

Was there a note of aggravation in her voice? Had "they"—the doctors and nurses who had been fighting against the clock, trying to figure out what was wrong with Shannon—simply been *annoying* Jeannine?

My lawyer asked, "Did you ever tell any of them that she had been scratched by something in the spring?"

"No. I never thought of it. It never crossed my mind."

How I hate this woman. I hate her for her lies, for the self-absorbed illusion she built around herself—an illusion she refused to lift even while her own daughter lay dying in a hospital bed; an illusion she refused to lift even after Shannon died.

Jeannine went on to recount her impressions of when we'd

learned that Shannon had rabies, and the events that followed. She over-elaborated on every answer, looking for sympathy and rising to her own defense very quickly. She never mentioned her convenient and frequent absences from the hospital all the while Shannon was there.

"They're saying that she told them she was bit by a bat," she said. "And I'm asking, 'What are you talking about? She wasn't bit by a bat, and she can't even talk. How can she tell you she was bit by a bat? She's on life support and can't speak.'"

"So the nurse was saying that Shannon told them that?" Jack verified.

"Yeah. That's what they said at first, that Shannon told them. And they just had me all confused."

Had this really happened? Had the nurses reported Shannon mentioning a bat bite? Or was this just another creation of Jeannine's addled mind?

"Was Pat there when they confronted you with that?"

"He was in the hallway, screaming that I killed her," she answered. "That I did it on purpose, and I killed her because she was his favorite one and I was happy now. He was screaming all the time."

She was right; I was. And I did say those things. And I wouldn't take one word back. In fact, I would have asked her, if I'd been the lawyer in this situation, why *she* hadn't been screaming as well at that point. After all, we'd just found out that our daughter had a potentially fatal disease.

"Is that when they gave her medication?" Jack asked.

Jeannine nodded. "They told us about the girl who had rabies and lived, and the experiment, and asked if we wanted to do it. And we did."

"Okay."

"And that sucks," Jeannine added, another of her nasty afterthoughts, "that I let my daughter be an experiment."

Jeannine went on about how terrible it was when Shannon was put in a coma, and how horrible it had been when she'd died. She painted a picture of herself as the bravest mother in the world, comforting her other children while Shannon's life support was turned off, while I waited out in the hallway, unable to watch my daughter die.

But my lawyer had enough sense to cut her off in the middle of her paean to her virtuous, righteous self. "You don't need to go any further on that," he told her. "That's fine."

Jeannine acquiesced with a quiet and very annoyed sounding, "Okay."

And after that, the deposition didn't last much longer. They covered the DCFS (Department of Children and Family Services) and state police investigations very briefly, and Jeannine was able to get in a few more digs at me and plenty more accolades for herself. When the whole thing was over, she and Jimmie simply got up and left, probably feeling pretty good about the lies they had told.

The next day, I met with my lawyer and got a briefing on the things that had been said, and my fury was renewed. When I went home, I felt exhausted, but anxious to get the whole thing over with. My trial was only four days away, and I couldn't wait.

CHAPTER TWENTY-SEVEN

On August 7, 2007, Jack Rosen and I showed up at the Porter Superior Court in Valparaiso, Indiana, prepared to do battle. My brother-in-law, Jerry, even flew in from California just to be there for me. I was more than ready to finally get this all over with.

Jeannine showed up with a small entourage—Jimmie, of course, his sister, Carla, and one of Jeannine's cronies, a skinny, drugged-out-looking woman who had no real reason for being there. Jimmie shuffled into the courtroom behind Jeannine and sat down with her at the counsel table. Still unable to afford an attorney, Jeannine had chosen to represent herself and I guessed that he was her poor excuse for an assistant.

The Honorable Jeffrey A. Jones was the judge in our case, and he started things off by asking my attorney, Jack, to set the record. This meant that Jack had to note aloud who was there and what the case was about. The judge then took stock of who was in the room, focusing his attention on the extra person at Jeannine's side.

"We've got too many people at counsel table," Jones told him. "Who are you, sir?"

"Jimmie Hackworth. I was subpoenaed."

"All right. You're going to have to wait outside until you're called to testify."

Yes! I already felt as though I'd won a small but satisfying victory.

When Jimmie had vacated the courtroom, the judge set about tending to some more formalities. "Have the parties completed our TransParenting program?" he asked.

"Yes," I answered, forgetting that I was supposed to let my lawyer speak for me.

"Yes," Jack said at just about the same time. Jeannine noted that she had as well.

"All right," Judge Jones went on. "I guess I'll address this to you, Mr. Rosen. This matter was set for a one-hour final contested hearing in 2004. How did we get from that to two days of whatever we're going to hear?"

I'd been wondering that myself; I knew the literal answer, the whys and hows of the delays we'd been put through so far. But *How did we get here?* was a question I still asked myself just about every day.

"There was a substantial change in circumstances wherein one of the children is deceased, and the question of custody then arose," Jack told the judge. "Prior to that, there had been pretty much a mutual understanding of joint legal, with physical custody already being established pursuant to the first mediation agreement that was filed with the court."

Jack and the judge went back and forth about this and other formalities for a while. They discussed a domestic relations case management order; Jack presented to the court a second mediation agreement; he also noted that he'd received a petition that morning for a contempt citation that Jeannine had filed on Friday, the day of her deposition. Seemed that she'd been concerned about some of the issues we were set to go over at the trial. Jack notified the court that we were ready to address all the issues that day.

There was also some talk about a subpoena Jack had sent out to Lynn Johnson of the State Police Department, asking her to come and testify about her investigative report. A lawyer had filed a motion to quash that subpoena, and Jack did not oppose it, as it was still an ongoing investigation.

Again, all formalities. And then finally, after what seemed like hours, we were ready to address the real issues of the trial.

Judge Jones asked Jack to present his case first, and he launched right into it, calling Jimmie Hackworth to the stand. Jimmie was brought back into the courtroom and sworn in, stating his name and address, and then he answered many of the same questions he'd been asked in his deposition: when he'd met my family and under what circumstances, where he'd lived, why he no longer had a driver's license. He answered questions about his relationship with Sam, Jeannine's relationship with Sam, his involvement in Sam's death and finally, when and how he and Jeannine had become—I guess you could call it *involved*.

"Were you and Jeannine doing any drinking?" Jack asked him, regarding the time when Jimmie was staying at my house with Jeannine and my children.

"No."

"Were you doing any drugs together?"

"No."

"So if the children were complaining to Mr. Carroll about marijuana being used and alcohol and things like that, that would not be correct?"

I shook my head. These allegations that my children had made—I knew that they were true. What reason did they have to lie? On the whole, I thought that I'd raised a pretty good family and my children knew right from wrong, and they were really bothered by things that they knew were wrong. When they'd told me about Jeannine and Jimmie smoking and drinking in the house while they were there, I had no reason not to believe them.

"It would not be correct," Jimmie said with a straight face, and I wondered how he could do it, especially given the laundry list of his own prescriptions he rattled off later in his testimony: Prozac, Xanax, Flexeril, Vicodin. He claimed that he didn't "self-medicate," but if that didn't prove that he did, then I didn't know what would.

Much of Jimmie's testimony covered what he'd gone over already in his deposition, and so for much of it I listened with only half an ear, my mind too focused on getting this done with and getting the custody issue resolved. None of the rest of it mattered—the divorce, the financial matters—they were all fairly meaningless to me. Nothing meant more than proving that Jeannine was a completely unfit caregiver for my three youngest children.

Fortunately, Jimmie gave me plenty of support on that front, in so many ways. First, he answered questions about Jeannine bringing the kids along on her overnight visits to Bourbon, where she and Jimmie had met for their trysts after the work was done on the Portage house.

"When they would come down to visit you in Bourbon," my lawyer asked, "where would they stay?"

"They would stay at the house," the jerk responded.

"At your house?"

"Yes. It was a studio apartment."

I couldn't help shaking my head. To think that my babies had to be holed up in one room with these two—and with whatever they were doing—just made my stomach turn.

"And when she would come down to visit you with the three younger children, where would the children sleep?" Jack asked.

"In bed," said Jimmie. "We slept on the couch."

According to his testimony, Jimmie and Jeannine moved around from place to place with Shannon, Mary and Kristine for the next year and a half or so. He wasn't great at remembering dates and addresses, or whether or not Jeannine had registered the girls for school. Shannon, he thought, was registered in at least one of the places they'd lived, but he never said a thing about whether or not she attended any classes.

The more Jimmie spoke, the more apparent it became to everyone in the room, I thought, that the life he lived with Jeannine was nothing but shady. Jeannine did not work at all, he testified, and he rarely did; sometimes, they lived off of some savings he claimed to have, but I didn't see how he could save a penny when he didn't even have a job through most of the year.

When asked about collecting welfare, the bum explained that neither he nor Jeannine received any while they were unemployed, but that Jeannine started filing for it once he was working again. Of course, she didn't claim his income on the forms, because she wanted to get the maximum benefit—surely not to use for the kids, but for whatever other habits of her own were sucking up all of her resources.

Now, this is another thing that gets me: the welfare system. I'm all for helping people out when they need it; everyone falls on hard luck sometimes, and there's nothing wrong with getting a little assistance 'til you can get back on your feet.

But you know, I pay my taxes, and the government distributes my money as it sees fit, which includes funneling it into the welfare system. Because of this, if I had a say, I would make every person applying for welfare take a drug test—and they would get nothing if they did not pass it. The rest of us have to take drug tests to apply for jobs, and to keep them, so what's the difference? You want money? Prove to me that you're going to use it to support your children, not to buy liquor and drugs. Show me that while I'm out working my ass off to pay for your welfare check, you're not at home getting high on my dime.

If Jeannine and Jimmie had been forced to take drug tests to get their money, I am quite sure that things would have turned out a lot differently. They never would have come up clean, and someone in authority would have seen just how unfit a mother Jeannine was, based on that. The girls would have been given to me, where they obviously would have been better off.

But that, of course, would never happen. The system is what it is, and it would take some sort of miracle for it to be overhauled at this point. I can keep hoping, and I can talk about it as loudly as I want, but until someone in authority steps up and does the right thing for the children involved, nothing will ever change.

So Jeannine got her welfare, and used it for God knew what. Even with that money and the food stamps she received, I was left wondering, how was she feeding the children? And paying rent or utilities? How could she and Jimmie afford the booze and drugs that he so vehemently denied they were using—even though I was pretty sure, from what my kids and former neighbors said, they still were?

"When was the last time you were picked up for public intoxication?" my lawyer asked at this point.

"July of last year," Jimmie answered proudly.

"July of '06?" Jack clarified, and Jimmie agreed that it was correct.

"And at what location were you picked up?" Jack went on.

"Quad Street." This was the site of his house, where he, Jeannine and the girls stayed much of the time.

"Had there been an altercation between you and Jeannine at the time?"

"Yes, sir, verbal."

"And did she, in fact, call the police to have them come to that location?"

"Yes, sir, she did."

Two completely sober people having a screaming match, ending with one of them calling the cops on the other? That didn't sound like sober behavior to me.

After he'd had a chance to spout off all the bullshit he wanted about his and Jeannine's irresponsible behavior, my lawyer gave Jimmie a chance to have his say about what had happened to Shannon. At first, he played dumb:

Q: Did the time come when there was an incident with Shannon in June of '06?

A: Possibly.

Q: Okay. Did you recall anything specifically that happened in June of '06 with Shannon?

A: Not specifically, no.

Q: Okay. Do you remember being told anything by Jeannine about Shannon in June of '06?

A: That she had woke her up the night before and that something had landed on her...

And then he launched into his very well rehearsed story about Shannon and the bird scratch—the one that Jeannine had told him about because, he alleged, he was sleeping at the time and neither heard nor saw a thing. He especially didn't see a bat, especially not on Shannon's arm. There was nothing here that he hadn't said at his deposition—as well as nothing that he *had* said in the media.

I was thinking in particular of his interview with the TV news station. To them, he'd quite freely talked about the bat story. That stuck in my head like a spike; he'd admitted that there had been a bat, just that one time, and thank God there had been a reporter there to hear it. Now, it was in print for the entire world to see.

Oh, but right, he was delusional at that point in time. He'd gone over all that in his deposition—his sarcoidosis, his hospitalization, his delusional state of mind. Now, my lawyer dug into him about this in a way that left me, in a word, very pleased.

"Are there any medical records that you've got to present to the court showing that, at that particular point in time, you were delusional?" Jack asked.

"Not that I was delusional, no."

Funny how he'd been admitted to a hospital and not one doctor, not even a nurse, had made a single note that he was not in his right mind due to his illness. Even funnier, my lawyer uncovered, was that Jimmie himself could not substantiate his own claim.

"When you did research on this disease," Jack asked, "did you go on the Internet?"

"My brother-in-law did. He pulled some stuff down off of the Internet, and so did my brother."

"Okay. And I believe you said that there wasn't anything in that on being delusional. Is that correct?"

"Anything could flare it up," Jimmie commented off-topic, but then conceded, "No, I seen nothing in it."

Later, on re-direct, Jack was really able to drive the last nail into it.

During her cross-examination, Jeannine had questioned Jimmie on her calling the house during Shannon's hospital stay and learning that there were reporters camped outside. Ever the good mother in her own eyes, Jeannine claimed that she had told Jimmie and Mark—and even one of the reporters herself—to go away and leave them all alone.

"You were asked questions," Jack reminded Jimmie on the re-direct, "concerning the phone call from Jeannine when you were, in fact, at your house and the TV people were there. Do you recall that?"

"Yeah."

"Do you recall the conversation with Jeannine?"

"I recall she called, wanting to talk to one of the reporters."

"Okay."

"I done that."

"Okay. Were you delusional when you were talking to Jeannine?"

I practically jumped up out of my chair and started cheering when my lawyer asked this. *Brilliant!* I thought, trying to maintain a calm demeanor.

Jimmie paused. "I don't know," he mumbled finally.

"You don't know." My lawyer nodded, taking his own pause for effect. "Is that the same time you talked to the reporter and told them about the bat on Shannon's arm?"

"Yes, sir," Jimmie answered, but the defiant note he'd had in his voice all along had disappeared. I can't say that I missed it.

Jeannine's cross-examination, by my attorney Jack Rosen, started out just as Jimmie's had. There were questions about her background—

maiden name, employment (or lack thereof), number and names of children. They talked about our joint custody and mediation agreements, about her relationships with Sam and Jimmie, and about the tattoos on her ass. Finally, they got to the topic of our children.

"Which children were registered for school in the fall of '04?" Jack asked her.

"In Portage—Mark, Barbara, Shannon. Mary went to pre-school."

"Did a time come when you were contacted by the school about any of the kids, concerning their lack of attendance?"

"I can't recall. If so, it might have been Mark. If they miss so many days, you get a letter in the mail stating that if it continues, you have to explain why. They didn't just stay home to stay home. When they stayed home, they were sick."

This was almost laughable. Jeannine hadn't been keeping Shannon out of school because she was sick; it was because Jeannine was too lazy to get the kids up on time in the morning. Maybe she'd gotten letters about Mark, too, who was older and could skip classes of his own free will, but as far as the younger kids were concerned, I was sure that any and all of their absences were due to Jeannine's poor parenting—not to illness.

I knew, at this point, exactly what "contact" from the school that my lawyer was referring to in his question to Jeannine—even if she wanted to pretend that *she* didn't know. A letter had been sent, about a month into that school year, stating that Shannon had only been attending one or two days a week, and that if it continued, the school administration would start some sort of investigation. I knew this because they had sent the letter to me as well. I always made sure, no matter where the kids were going to school, that my address was in their files, and that I was copied on any correspondence the school sent out.

And though Jeannine chose not to remember it at the moment, I knew the outcome of that letter very well: Shannon had been sent to school every day from that point on. The word "investigation," to Jeannine, was a red flag that she did not want to mess with.

"In the fall of '04, what grade was Shannon in?" Jack asked.

"Maybe second—second or third, I'm not positive, actually."

What a great mother—couldn't even remember what grade her daughter had been in three years earlier.

"At that point in time, Pat was out of the house, correct?" Jack asked.

"That's correct."

"And it would have been your responsibility to see that the second-grader would be going to school?"

"Yes."

Still, she saw nothing wrong with the fact that she had kept the kids out of school so often. I could read it on her face: she felt perfectly justified in everything that she'd done.

And that was pretty much the attitude she went through the entire testimony with. Everything she said had an air of righteousness about it, as though she were the only one in the room who had an ounce of sense in her. Whether she was talking about the house going into foreclosure, the health department being called on her while she was running her so-called day care, or getting Mary tested for ADHD, she was the hero of every story; she was the only one who seemed to be doing anything about anything. And I, of course, was the villain whenever possible.

An example: "Did you list Pat as a person to contact in case there was an emergency at school?" Jack asked her.

"I would think that I did," answered Jeannine.

"Do you know if you did or not?"

"I'm not positive." What a lie. "He makes sure he lists himself for everything, anyhow."

Damn right I did. If she wasn't going to do it, then I made sure that I did it myself. I had every right to be notified if and when something was wrong with one of my children while they were at school.

"I'm sorry," Jack said, "I don't understand."

Jeannine just about rolled her eyes, as if Jack were an idiot for not seeing how incredibly evil and sneaky my behavior was. "He makes sure he gets himself in there, anyhow," she said slowly, pointedly. "Whether I do it or not."

"Well, you sound somewhat resentful that he would take an active role in the kids' school activities. Is that what you mean?"

She said, "No," then went on to complain that I never helped the kids with their homework on the weekends I had them. This was true, in part, but mainly because they didn't often bring any schoolwork with them. I did keep them as active as possible—reading books, doing arts and crafts—but there was only so much I could do in the limited time I was allowed with them. The sixteen hours of driving I had to do each weekend just to see them—four hours each way, on Friday and then again on Sunday—sort of put a damper on things.

Much of Jeannine's testimony was a repeat of her deposition—especially what she had to say about Shannon's so-called bird scratch. That story sounded so rehearsed by then, I didn't know how anyone could have believed her. Jack did ask her a lot more questions concerning her *other* parenting failures, including letting the children's state-funded health care lapse, not following up on a therapy recommendation for Mary and leaving our two youngest children at a friend's house for an entire month—all the while having several medical procedures done on herself, and always making sure that she had enough of her own "medication" to get her through the day.

Perhaps the most telling thing she said the entire time, however, was when Jack questioned her about attending Shannon's funeral. "Did you help make arrangements for your daughter's funeral?" he led off with.

And Jeannine responded, "Over the phone," which was a bit of a stretch. "Pat told me what he was doing, and I told him that I thought he was doing a good job," which did not constitute actually *helping*.

"And you attended that, correct?" Jack asked next.

"Unfortunately, I did," Jeannine answered, and my jaw nearly hit the floor. *Unfortunately* she went to her daughter's funeral? Was she insane? Was she saying that she would have rather just stayed home?

"It was very difficult," she concluded. "I would have been content with a memorial service."

Right, so you wouldn't have to look at Shannon's body, and see what you'd done! I thought, grabbing the arms of my chair so that I wouldn't jump up and rush the witness stand. I couldn't believe the bullshit that was coming out of that woman's mouth. I only hoped that the judge would hear it, too, and that he would see Jeannine for the person that she really was.

When Jeannine was through, I was called up to the stand myself, and boy was I ready to have my say. I was sworn in, given the whole opening routine like the others had been—name, address, employment, all that—and then questioned about many of the topics that had already been covered: Sam, Jimmie and Jeannine; the financial matters surrounding our divorce settlement; Jeannine's moving around with the kids; their health issues; the fact that they barely lived above the poverty line.

And then at last, I got to air all the dirty laundry I had been saving up on Jeannine for so long.

"Are you concerned," my lawyer began, "about the economics of Jeannine's home?"

"Very much," I responded, making the understatement of the year.

"In what respects?"

"I think my children live just about at the poverty level, if they don't live *in* the poverty level. There's no income, there's no work. It's—the kids don't have anything new. I don't like the fact that the children are basically growing up in poverty."

"If they lived with you, would they live at that level?"

"Absolutely not. I think my economic future is much brighter. I have much more to offer the children in that regard."

"Are you concerned," Jack went on, "with the number of health care issues that Jeannine has, and how that may impact your children?"

"Absolutely. She has quite a few illnesses. Doctor visits, hospital stays, surgeries… It's just constant. And I don't know how she can care for the children and take care of all that."

"Are you also concerned about Jimmie Hackworth, who lives there?"

"Absolutely." No doubt, he was one of the biggest concerns on my mind.

"What are your concerns, Pat?" Jack asked, giving me the chance to elaborate.

"I don't know him from Adam. He's done time in prison. You know, he doesn't work, he had drinking issues, and he's raising my daughters. Would you want your daughters—I shouldn't ask you the questions, you're asking me the questions—but I don't think any man wants his daughter in that situation."

I sat back in my seat, my head fuming. Just talking about that loser made me angry, but I had to hold it together. I couldn't lash out. I just had to answer the questions and get through this without breaking up.

"Seeing Sam and Jimmie and some of these other decisions," Jack then asked me, "are you concerned that this decision making process that Jeannine engages in is not in the best interests of these children?"

"Absolutely. Absolutely."

"Do you think it's in the best interests of these children that she took them, at some point in time, from Portage to visit him in Bourbon or whatever other little town it was, while she was still married to you?"

I paused. How was I supposed to answer that? "Yes," seemed like too obvious a response. "It seems," I said instead, "that every decision she makes, the children are put at risk. My children are put at risk every single day with her."

I could see Jeannine scowling at me from her counsel table, and it was all I could do to not stand up and tell her to wipe that nasty look right off her face. I felt like I was fighting for my life here—for my children's lives—while to her, it was all some kind of game.

Jack went into a line of questioning then about things that had happened while Shannon had been in the hospital, about how and when we'd found out that she'd had rabies.

"This incident with Shannon," he went on to say. "Has that caused you to question the decision making of Jeannine?"

"I've always questioned the decision making of Jeannine," I answered quickly. "When I think something else can't possibly go wrong, it does. I mean, her decision making has been poor for quite a while."

"If this Court were to order that there be some counseling between yourself and Jeannine and the children, to work through some of the tragedy here, would you participate?"

"If the Court ordered it, yes. I think the children and myself need counseling. If I get the children, I will certainly do that. If Jeannine's involved, that would have to be through a court."

And that was no lie. If I would ever have to say a direct word to her again, it would be by the order of a judge.

CHAPTER TWENTY-EIGHT

Since Jeannine had no lawyer of her own, when it came time for my cross-examination, she stepped up to do it herself. I took a deep breath and tried to prepare myself for what would undoubtedly be a lot of grandstanding and nonsense.

I do have to give her credit, because she did hold her own in the courtroom the entire two days we were there. However, it wasn't long before my cross—which started out with a lengthy nitpicking of some of the more boring aspects of our divorce-related financial issues—devolved into something reminiscent of the fights we'd had in the past, minus a lot of the cursing.

"When Shannon was in the hospital," Jeannine started out with, "and you informed me that you were picking up the kids and that you were taking them and I would not be getting them back, you stated that you were questioning my everything. How often did Mary and Kristine see Charles and Sara and Cassie and Roger?"

I tried not to smirk at the not-quite-sneaky way she tried to get her own testimony into the question. Yes, I'd questioned "her everything"—that is, everything about her, everything she was doing—and I still feel that it was the right thing for me to do. But she seemed now to be saying it as if it were ridiculous, as if I were ridiculous for questioning anything she did.

"Very rarely," I answered.

"And that was November. October, that was the month of October. What grade was Mary in?"

"Second."

"Was she attending school in Bourbon?"

"Yes, she was."

"Are you aware that she's very active in church?"

"I know that you've sent them on a bus once a week to church, yes." It was a blunt answer, but an honest one.

"And that's all you're aware of about their church?"

I wanted to say, *I'm aware that you put them on that bus so that they'll be out of your hair for three hours every Sunday*, but thought better of it. "That's all you tell me about that," I said instead. "I don't know what church they go to, I don't know what religion it is. I wasn't made aware of that."

And with that, Jeannine just let the floodgates open.

"And you thought it would be better for Mary and Kristine to be with family that they see a couple of times a year and not be in school and not go to church and not be in their neighborhood than to be where I had placed them with my friends, going to school, going to church on Sunday, without their routine being disrupted any more than it already was with Shannon in the hospital?"

As she stood there glaring at me, I paused, wondering if she was done or if she was only stopping to catch her breath. When it appeared that she was waiting for my answer, I gave it to her: "Yes. As a parent, I was exercising my right. Should either parent not be able to care for the children, they're supposed to be placed with another person. The other parent is supposed to be told immediately where they are, with a phone number and address, which you never provided to me when Mary and Kristine were with your friends, who I don't know. You know your sister, you know my brother. I took it upon myself to decide that they would be much better off there. Mary is in second grade, and she was being home-schooled by your sister, Cassie, a high school teacher, and by Sara. Mary did quite well and Kristine even learned to write her name."

We glared at each other again. It felt like we were right back in the kitchen of the house in Portage, hurling insults and accusations at one another, never seeing eye to eye.

"Was there a curriculum at that time for home-schooling?" she finally asked, changing the subject, as she usually did when someone said something that she did not like or agree with.

This was how much of the cross-examination went: she would hurl long-winded, convoluted accusations, harp on irrelevant details and, occasionally, give me the opportunity to get in a good dig or two myself.

"How do you know that we live at the poverty level?" she asked in one instance.

"It's pretty obvious," I responded. "You don't work. Jimmie works very sporadically. Your utility bills are being paid by the church. You get financial help everywhere you turn. You're on public assistance. That's pretty much at poverty level, if you ask me."

Another time: "How do you know that the kids don't ever get anything new?"

"The kids tell me. Whenever they get something, I ask them where they got it. They say your friends or somebody else got it for them, or they got it from the church. Any clothes they have, basically, I've bought them. You send them to me in clothes that are ill-fitting and old. I see my kids—they don't have many luxuries."

Later on, completely out of the blue, she came out with, "Why do you think Barbara has so much animosity toward me?"

I had to stop and think. A second earlier, she'd been trying to grill me on what town I worked in. Then, this. *Well*, I figured, *she asked—I might as well go for it.*

"In my honest opinion," I began, "you basically abandoned her in the middle of eighth grade. You left to go live with your boyfriend and you told the other kids to go wherever they pleased, and she chose to come with me. Barbara has lost out on quite a bit. You gave her up for your boyfriend. You asked the question—that's your answer."

"Do you encourage Barbara that it would be important for her to have a relationship with her mother?"

"No. I leave that up to Barbara. She's seventeen years old. That's totally up to her, what she does."

"You never encouraged her to spend time with her mom?"

"Every time Barbara would go to your house, which was very seldom, she came home really—just very upset. She does not like your boyfriend. She does not like your living arrangement. She does not like your lifestyle. And she does not want anything to do with it."

"What is my lifestyle?" There we go...turning it all around to herself at last.

"I don't know. It's not normal."

"What's normal?"

"Getting out of bed in the morning, taking care of your family, having a job, paying your bills. That's my opinion of normal."

Jeannine was able to go on bickering with me for another half hour or so before the judge decided to call it a day and adjourned the trial until the next day.

As the judge dismissed the courtroom, everyone stood up and I noticed Jeannine's brother, Jerry, in the audience, standing dangerously close to Jimmie Hackworth. Jimmie was winking at Jerry and leering with a big, stupid grin on his face—the same look he had been giving me. I could see Jerry's face turning red.

Great, I thought, my mind exhausted. *Just what we need right now—a fight in the courtroom.* Jerry was a tough ex-Marine, and nobody to screw with. I wished that the jerk would just leave the rest of us alone and go home.

The two glared at each other for a minute longer, and then Jimmie put his hand up to his face, scratching his cheek as though he had an itch—but doing it with his middle finger, aimed directly at Jerry. He blew Jerry a kiss as well, and I knew that it would be all over from there.

Jerry stepped over to Jimmie and put a hand up in his face. "I have five Irish fingers here, buddy. One of them is for you," he said, giving Jimmie a look that could have killed him. At that point, Jimmie's trampy-looking, speed-addicted sister, Carla, decided to get involved.

"Let's take this outside!" she started yelling. "Come on! Come on!"

It was easy to see that Jerry wanted to haul back and hit Jimmie, but he restrained himself, and just in time: As Carla continued to scream, two police officers who had been watching through the courtroom's glass doors barreled in to break it up. They got in between Jimmie and Jerry and separated them, and then escorted the jerk, his sister and Jeannine out of the building.

On August 8, 2007, our hearing resumed, and Jeannine continued with cross-examining me. We talked a lot about Barbara—her schooling, an accident she'd had recently, a possible diagnosis of ADHD. She tried to get me worked up with some inflammatory topics—an allegation (completely false) that at some point, I'd struck Mary and given her a black eye; a couple of temporary bouts of depression I'd suffered when she'd threatened me with divorce in the past; the time I'd called 911 on Peter in Oak Lawn, because he'd been drunk and belligerent and I could not calm him down.

And then predictably, everything for Jeannine returned to money and material things. She spent he remainder of my cross asking me about the house, things I'd paid for, wallpaper in the bathrooms, repairs that I'd never done. She focused so much on the tangible aspects of the case, and so little on the emotional ones— the children, what had happened to Shannon—that I wondered if it was all the same to her in the end. If Shannon's death affected her less than not getting her "fair share" of the proceeds from the sale of our house.

By the time she was done with me, I practically stumbled off the stand. I felt exhausted, frustrated and disgusted. I was more than ready for the trial to be over with—but first, we had two more witnesses to question.

First came Elaine, our neighbor back in Portage. Elaine and I had maintained a good relationship even after I'd been kicked out of the house; Jeannine and Elaine, not so much. She detailed many of the reasons for their animosity during my lawyer's direct examination.

"Did a time come when that friendship started to wane or fall apart?" Jack asked her, referring to her relationship with Jeannine.

"Yes," Elaine answered. "The last time we spoke, Peter, the son, came to my house and was concerned about Jeannine's drug use."

"Can you give me a time on this, please?"

"Within a year of their separation."

"Okay. And what took place?"

"I pretty much knew that was going to be the end of our relationship if I confronted her on this."

"Did you then talk to Jeannine about that?"

"Yes. I told her that Peter was concerned about her drug use. He was very upset about it. He asked me to talk to her about it. When I spoke with her, she explained what each drug did, that they were all prescribed to her and that she didn't have a problem. And that was the end of the conversation and our friendship."

"Why did that conversation seem to end your relationship with her?"

"Because if you confront Jeannine on anything, your relationship is over."

You got that right, I thought. That was Jeannine's M.O.: no matter who you were, if you called her on her bad behavior, you were gone. Dead to her. Cut out of her life forever.

Jack asked Elaine about Jimmie, then, and about the time she'd called the cops on him for building an enormous bonfire in the yard. She also testified that he had called her then-thirteen-year-old son a "little faggot"; later, during cross-examination, Jeannine tried to feebly defend this sort of bullying by bringing up the son's ADD and behavioral problems, as if that had anything to do with it.

Elaine was open and honest with her testimony, especially when it came to stressing what a dangerous environment my two youngest daughters were living in.

"Did you ever observe either Mary or Kristine wandering the neighborhood without parental supervision?" my lawyer asked her.

"Yes," said Elaine. "During the summer, we'd spend a lot of time in our backyard, and we would hear Mary's high-pitched screaming. The two would be just wandering around the corner area, which is about three or four houses down from their own. At eleven o'clock at night."

"And what, if anything, in regards to that, did you do?"

"Shannon would usually go chase them down, or Barbara. There was one time when I had to call Jeannine because Mary was outside at one in the morning."

"You called Jeannine?"

"Yes, and she didn't answer. Pete was out there, so I told him to bring her back in the house, and he did, but she wandered back out. I told him again, and he did it. And then she came back out. So I went and knocked on her door and got Jeannine and told her what was going on."

"And Mary would have been about how old at that point?"

Elaine did not even have to pause to figure it out. "Three or four."

I shook my head. My poor little girls. Anything could have happened to them had Elaine not been keeping an eye out; they could have been hit by a car, or kidnapped, or worse.

Elaine went on to relate some information about the many times she'd seen the girls unsupervised around the above-ground pool in the Portage house's backyard. After one incident—one of many, I guessed—she'd called the Department of Children and Family Services. When Jack asked her why, she replied: "Because I felt the kids needed help. I felt the kids needed to be protected. I felt they were being neglected."

Jeannine's cross-examination of Elaine did not bring anything new to light; it was interesting only because Jeannine's dislike of the woman was so apparent, it was almost laughable. Her tone of voice was acidic, but her questions failed at every turn. In the end, the judge admonished her for making inquiries that were outside the scope of direct examination and with that, predictably, Jeannine ended her questioning.

The next and final witness was Sara Carroll, my sister-in-law, whose testimony was mainly about the few weeks that Mary and Kristine had spent with her while Shannon was in the hospital. Sara's answers were calm and kind; she only had positive things to say about the girls and about the time she'd spent with them. She talked about home schooling them, teaching Kristine to write her name, regulating how much TV they watched and saying prayers with them every night. It sounded like such an idyllic existence, so completely opposite of what the girls were used to at home; just knowing that they'd had even a short time like that, a time free of worries and fear, made me feel pretty good.

But in reality, I guess it wasn't all so perfect. No matter where they were, the girls had a dark side that they carried with them; when asked if Mary and Kristine ever talked to her about their home in Bourbon, Sara replied, "Kristine would start to talk about home life or say something like, 'At home, we did…' And Mary would tell her, 'Stop. No. Don't.' And Kristine would be quiet."

This infuriated me. They'd all been trained to act like that, to keep whatever happened at home a secret. I wondered what sort of nightmares those two little girls kept from me even then; I wondered what Shannon would have told me in the past, had she not been forbidden to do so.

And then came the most heartbreaking story of all.

"Did they ever talk to you about Shannon being bit by a bat or a bird or anything?" Jack asked.

"There was one instance," Sara began. "When we would go to bed, they were in unfamiliar surroundings, so to make it homier for the girls, we would have—they called it a pajama party. They were in their jammies and underneath the covers, and I would lie across the bottom of the bed. After we said our prayers, the lights would be off and we would talk. One night, they had prayed for Mom and Dad and for Shannon, that she would be better. And Kristine, who was very animated, said, 'I was so scared when that happened to Shanny.' And I said, 'Well, I bet you were. It was pretty scary.' And she said, 'They came running upstairs, and Shanny was screaming and Mom threw a blanket over her and ran into the bathroom and shut the door.' I said, 'Well, Mom had to attend to what happened to Shanny.'

"And Kristine said, 'That's why we hate bats.'"

Jeannine's cross-examination of Sara was pretty much entirely unnecessary. She had Sara repeat the story that Kristine had told her about the night the bat bit Shannon—and that was it. Whatever point Jeannine was trying to make, I didn't see it at all. I didn't see how anyone could.

There was a recess then and when we returned, the judge asked Jack Rosen some questions about child support and the mediation agreement between Jeannine and myself. He also talked to Jeannine about her current usage of methadone—she said she hadn't used any in "probably" three months—and about her inability to work, and her application for disability. Then, he called for closing arguments.

Jack went first and made a very professional and logical presentation to the judge that summarized the points of the case and stressed, above all else, the importance of the custody issue. "What we've been talking about for the last day and a half is what is in the best interests of Mary and Kristine. We have painted for this Court a picture of two little girls who have been in a disruptive living circumstance for a good number of years."

Most of his speech centered on Jeannine's questionable behavior, the dysfunctional environment that she willfully raised the children in and the contrasting, stable environment that I could provide for them. "We would ask the Court to find that based on the evidence that's been presented, the dad is the person who can provide for these children's best interests. He, in fact, *wants* that opportunity and is concerned that if he doesn't have these children, there could be another Shannon."

Jeannine's summation wasn't nearly so thoughtful or elegant. She rambled on and on about herself, mostly, in a, "why can't we all just get along?" tone that grated on every nerve in my body. "I did not want to continue throwing stones," she said at one point, talking about how if she'd really wanted to, she could have had a lawyer and gotten things to work out "to her advantage."

"I did not want to continue any more arguing, any more allocating, any more proving." Oh, Saint Jeannine, you are truly pious indeed…

Through the course of her babbling, she managed to mention that she'd never heard "the bat story" until someone from the Department of Children and Family Services had told her about it. She also said, in a roundabout way, that Sara Carroll was lying about the bat story Kristine had told her. Was this Jeannine's defense?

"Kristine said that she was scared when it happened and that I rushed into a bathroom. Well, there is no bathroom up there. You have to come down the stairs, through the house, back that way into the bathroom."

Strong argument, Jeannine, I thought. *Really proved your innocence there.*

When she started talking about how much Jimmie loved the kids—and how much they loved him right back—my mind started to tune her out. It was garbage, all of it, and listening to it only made me mad.

"I am willing to do whatever is possible so that we can communicate on what is good for the kids," she said in closing, referring to communicating with me. "I never deny him time with the kids. If he wants more time with them, I think he deserves it. I just ask that you make a fair judgment based on what has been submitted."

As she went back and took a seat behind her table, I wondered if she was sincere in that last statement. Did she really want what was fair, or was she just trying to pull at the heartstrings of the judge—a stranger who didn't know her and didn't know how manipulative she could be? Would he fall for her lies, or could he see through her well enough to know that as a mother, she was a ticking time bomb, and my children were right in the potential path of destruction?

"What I think this case cries out for," the judge said during his own closing, "probably as much as anyone I've heard in my eighteen years up here, is a child custody valuation, and I don't want to make anybody wait any longer. I do find, based on your testimony, that your marriage is irretrievably broken and should be dissolved, and I will restore you to the status of unmarried persons. As soon as I review these exhibits and digest the testimony a little further, I'll give you a ruling, I hope by next week, on the rest of it. In the meantime, the provisional orders continue and the agreements are approved and adopted as part of the Court's order. Thank you. Good luck, folks."

CHAPTER TWENTY-NINE

The judge's good-luck wish at the end of the trial turned out to be the most ironic aspect of the entire ordeal, because it seemed like only luck would bring me an answer. Though he had promised to make a decision on who would retain custody of Mary and Kristine by the following week, he failed to do so—and the same went for the week after that, and the week after that, and the week after that.

In fact, five months after I had my day in court, I had not heard one bit of news from the judge's office. Despite the fact that one of my daughters died while in Jeannine's custody, my two youngest children remained with her while the Court dragged its feet. Every day, I woke up worried for my little girls' safety, and every night I went to bed frustrated that there was nothing I could do to help them. The rest of the day, all the hours in between, I spent praying that they would be alright.

The longer this went on, the more I felt as though it wasn't just the judge who was being slow; it must have been a systemic problem as well. Much of the time, I thought that if I had been a mother petitioning for custody of her children, to get them away from an abusive father, I'd have had them with me that day, before the end of the trial. Conversely, if Shannon had died under the same circumstances while in my custody, I believed I would have been in jail long ago.

There was no doubt in my mind that the court system in Indiana, and throughout the rest of the United States, was biased against men who wanted custody of their children—even if we were obviously more fit to parent them than the mothers in question. Based on the response I'd gotten from the court by that point, what else could I think?

The Valparaiso University law school—regarded as a pretty good one—ran a hotline to give out free legal advice. While still waiting for my verdict, I asked a friend of mine to call them, to see what kind of help we could get.

Deciding that it would be best for us all to remain anonymous, my friend told the woman who answered the phone—a law student, no doubt, working on some extra credits—that her "brother" had gone to court a couple of months back for custody of his children, and had not yet received a ruling.

Without missing a beat, the woman on the other end asked, "This doesn't happen to be Judge Jones, does it? He's notoriously slow."

That, I thought, was the understatement of the year. Days, weeks and even months had passed and I still did not have a ruling in my custody case, though it hadn't been for my own lack of trying. Not one to just sit by and wait, I'd done everything I could think of to speed the process along, including phone calls, emails and talking about it to anyone who would listen. I'd called the judge's office so many times that his secretary told my lawyer I was a nuisance and needed to leave her alone. Jack, I was sure, knew what a nuisance I could be as well, as I called and emailed him routinely, asking for updates and advice on what to do.

And his answer, all along, was the same: Though the wait was frustrating, it was not unusual for the Court. He'd even seen cases like mine dragged out for nine months or more, and the thought of that just made me cringe.

As far as what I could do to make the judge work a little faster, believe me, I investigated every option. I even considered filing a "lazy judge" petition, which would have forced him to make a ruling immediately, but decided not to do it for fear that it would piss him off. My lawyer told me that if the judge did not like my filing, he could decide to rule against me when otherwise, he might not; he could also recuse himself from the case altogether—which would mean going back to court and doing the trial all over again. Honestly, I just didn't have that in me.

"The Court rules when it decides," Jack wrote me in an email. "Is this unusual? No, it is not for this Court."

What it came down to, then, was that I had no choice but to wait, and so I remained at the mercy of the Court. If I tried to force a ruling out of it, I risked losing everything I'd worked for so far, and though I wanted to do all I could to get my kids away from Jeannine as quickly as possible, I did not want to take too many chances. I was afraid of pissing off the Court, afraid that if I said or did the wrong thing, it would work against me—as if the Court wasn't already working against me enough.

On January 25, 2008, almost six full months after the court hearing, my phone rang. Caller ID told me that it was my lawyer; expecting it to be another "yes, we're still waiting" update, I considered just letting it go to voicemail. But then, I picked it up. *Might as well get it over with*, I told myself.

"Hi, Jack," I said wearily, settling myself down in a chair, waiting for the inevitable lack of news.

"Pat," my lawyer said on the other end of the line. "You won."

At first, I didn't know what he was talking about. But then... "I won?" I asked him meekly, afraid that I'd misheard him. But no, I hadn't—he repeated the phrase, then told me that he'd just gotten word from the Court, and that Judge Jones had granted me custody of my daughters. I didn't know what to say. I wanted to get up out of my chair and jump for joy, but I was afraid that my legs would give out if I tried.

After all those months of waiting, I couldn't believe that it was finally over, and that things had actually gone the way I'd wanted them to. I'd thought all along that the Court would rule against me; how often did custody go to a father, even when the mother was unfit to take care of herself, let alone her kids? But now they were mine—Mary and Kristine were mine, they would live with me and be safe. I thanked God over and over again.

When I was able to speak, I got the rest of the details from my lawyer. I would pick up Mary and Kristine from Jeannine's house on February 2, a Saturday, one week and one day later. It might as well have been a year; I wanted them with me that minute, that moment. I just hoped that Jeannine wouldn't try anything to mess it up in the meantime.

But of course, she did. Though she still didn't have a lawyer representing her, within a few days, she got one, and filed a motion with the Court to stop the transfer. Mary and Kristine were doing well in school, she said, and didn't want to live with their dad. Of course, I knew that this was far from the truth, and it seemed like a really weak defense. I found that I had little worry about her winning.

Excited about the girls' impending arrival, I made sure my apartment was in order, and arranged with my boss to adjust my hours for the first week, just until the girls got used to their new routine—and so that I could get used to it, too. During the week, I didn't hear anything from my lawyer about Jeannine's motion, so I called her and reminded her that I'd still be picking them up on Saturday, at noon. I asked her if she was going to give me a problem and she said, "We'll see," and then hung up.

The Court closed at 4:00 p.m. on the afternoon of Friday, February 1, and since she had not gotten a response to her motion yet, Jeannine resigned herself to giving the girls to me. She asked for a little more time with them, so I gave her until six o'clock.

When I finally went to get Mary and Kristine, they seemed excited to be coming with me. They knew what was going on, in a vague way—that they'd be coming to live with Daddy, that they wouldn't be living with Mommy anymore—and though I tried not to read too much into their expressions, I could tell that they were happy. I want to say that they seemed relieved. Maybe they were. I know I would have been.

On Monday, my lawyer called to see if there had been any drama with Jeannine when I'd picked up the girls. Surprisingly, I told him, there hadn't been. Jeannine was even being somewhat nice to me since then, which I was sure hinged on the fact that she no longer had our any of our children. Without them, she couldn't torment me with her erratic behavior, with her refusal to take care of them the way she should. She had nothing to hang over me anymore. In short, she had no control.

During the week, Jack called again to let me know that the Court had finally denied Jeannine's motion to stop the transfer of the girls. I'd expected it, but at last, I felt like we were free.

Mary and Kristine settled into their "new" home right away, and started at their new schools on Monday—Kristine in kindergarten and Mary in second grade. Sweet girls that they are, I don't doubt that they'll make new friends pretty quickly. Words cannot express how happy I am to have them with me on a daily basis. I'm Mr. Mom now, and I accept the responsibility. In fact, I'm thrilled to have it.

My two youngest daughters are safe now, and that's what matters. They will have opportunities in life; they will not grow up in poverty. They also have their older siblings around to look after them. For the first time in what has seemed like a very long time, I feel like we're a big, happy family again. I just wish that Shannon could be here to enjoy this good time with us.

This book may make it seem as though I have the world's largest chip on my shoulder against my ex-wife and aim to smear her name and make her life miserable—while making some money for myself in the process. I am not trying to profit from my daughter's death, though I can see where someone reading this book might think that.

But anyone who knows me can attest that none of it is true. I would never, ever seek to make money from what happened to Shannon; in fact, I would give all I have and then some just to have her back with me and her brothers and sisters. I would give anything to spend just five more minutes with her, to tell her that I love her one more time.

The purpose of this book, then, is simply to tell Shannon's story; to open people's eyes to the injustices in the US legal system, the prejudices that exist against fathers seeking custody of their children; and to show the world how devastating the consequences of one person's bad choices—including prescription drug abuse and alcoholism—can be. I just want the truth to come out.

So, no, I'm not looking to make money for myself off of this, so that I can live a life of ease on the back of my daughter's untimely death. Instead, I will use all of my earnings from this publication to make the lives of my other children better. I know that we all need professional help to understand and deal with everything that we have gone through, and that is my number-one priority. This book, as I see it, is Shannon's legacy and the only hope my family has to make a positive difference in all of our lives.

For further updates on my case, to purchase additional copies of this book or to comment on anything you've read here, please visit www.RabiesMom.com.